TREETS

A FEAST OF
FAMILY TREES

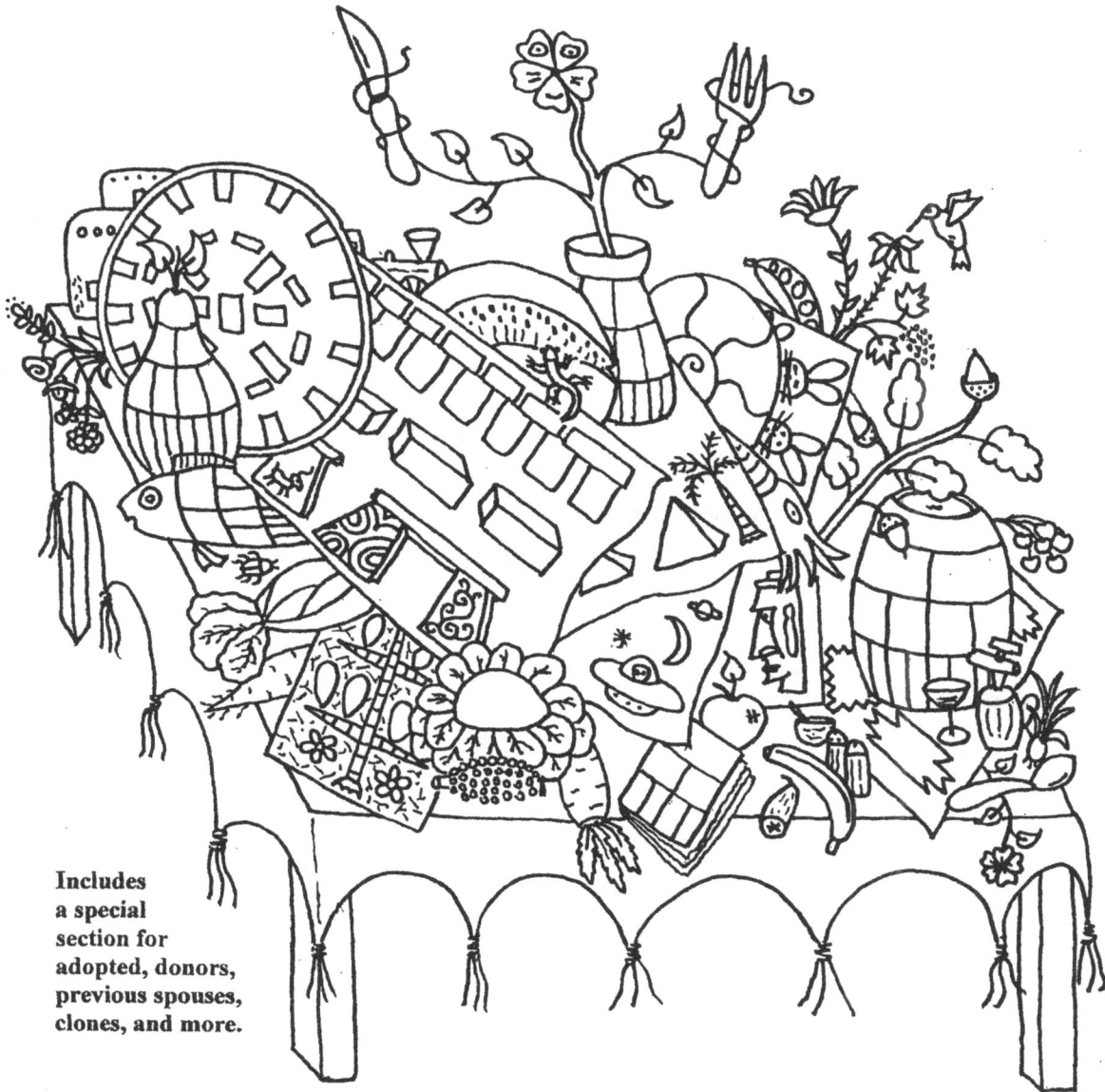

**Includes
a special
section for
adopted, donors,
previous spouses,
clones, and more.**

TONY MATTHEWS

CLEARFIELD

Printed for
Clearfield Company, Inc., by
Genealogical Publishing Co., Inc.
Baltimore, Maryland
2006

International Standard Book Number: 0-8063-5314-7

This book is
respectfully
dedicated to:

ALICE
+
SHEILA,

the best
of aunts.

TREETS.

Family Tree designing is a funny business. You might think that it is just one tiny corner of this world, but in fact it covers the entire world, for it is about people. And people are everywhere. And each is an individual.

When you consider Tony's First Law Of Family Trees that states :
A Family Tree Doesn't Have To Look Like A Tree you are opening a mental door that lets you into a whole new way of seeing things.

Then if you consider Tony's Second Law : *Even Truckers Have Families,* suddenly whole vistas are opened out before you. Let me explain.

First of all, the concept of a tree is a sort of misnomer, particularly if you put yourself at the bottom of a tree, with your ancestors forming the branches. That's back to front, or upside down, as it were, for your ancestors are your roots, while you are a branch from them. So why were they called Trees ? It's just the shape. They could have been called (river) deltas or tributaries.

What a Tree really is in fact is an organized body of information, and simply that. The 1-2-4-8-16-32 etc. line up of you, 2 parents, 4 grandparents etc. is old, obvious, works well, and is still mostly valid. Mind you, were you to put your name at the top of a page, then fill in your ancestors below, it would form a pyramid shape. Wonder why those ancient Egyptians didn't figure that one out ?

Do you even have to start at the top or bottom ? Not in my world ! You can go from the left hand side of the page, just like regular writing, and many charts do this. Still, if you were left handed, then starting from the right would feel somehow.....right. Then there's the middle, for you are truly the centre of your universe. We could even move into the third dimension and be talking about starting at the back or the front.

Feeling rebellious ?

Of course you could also ignore my first Law and design a Tree that looks like a tree....but would it be an oak, willow, fig, baobab, or pine ? One might well have special meaning for you, for example the pecan tree with an old tractor tyre that you swung on as a kid. Try drawing it, and put your name in the tyre.

I have shown many such different ways of setting up a Tree in my previous books ''Papertrees'', ''Creativitree'', and "Memory Trees" (from GPC and Clearfield), so won't describe them again here, merely use them. You will easily see how they work, and how they can even form patterns. I will, however, do an up-dated version of such things as how to fill in a Tree. Those of you nice people that have my other books may still find some new ideas here.

Patterns are from one side of the brain, the science and mathematics of form and shape. Your information does need this basic organization so that future generations will be able to quickly and correctly access your facts. However, Tree designing requires the use of the whole brain, with the other side providing the artistic ideas. In fact I often sit and argue with myself as I try to balance the need for good writing spaces against the desire for decoration.

You are unique.

But let's move on to the Second Law. I was selling Trees at a genealogical society, and a lady was enthusiastically looking at the many designs, and exclaiming how beautiful they were. Meanwhile, her husband was standing just outside the booth, with his arms folded, looking thoroughly bored. I asked the lady if her husband was not interested in Trees, and she replied " Oh, he's just a trucker. " When I got home that day I sat down and drew a Tree made up of trucks.....and immortalized the unknowing husband into my Second Law.

The point is that we are all different, with whole worlds of different careers, hobbies, interests, characteristics, and so on. My idea is that we can use these features in creating an individual Tree for each person and/or family. The concept is simple, for all that you have to do is to think of an image, or better still several images, that describe you. If you are a carpenter you might think of a saw, hammer, nails, screwdriver, glue bottle, drill, sawhorse, clamp, spirit level, t-square, ruler, pencil, chisel, router, and so on. It's that simple.

Not a mathematician ?

An important thing to say here, before I scare you off : is that you don't have to be either a mathematician or an artist to do a decent Tree. You could just copy one of mine (for your personal use, but not for profit or gain), or use one of the blanks that I'll include, or you can follow my designs using little more than ruler, pencil and graph paper to get the layout.....then you are ready for the images.

Where I've used vegetables, you might prefer fruit. Your grapes or orchids might be more appropriate than my roses. I'm sure that the botanists amongst you will notice that some of my so-called roses have only 4 petals. Is this important ? On a botanist's Tree yes, but it's not so necessary on a simple design. I'm just an idea person, not a real artist, so simply try to show what might be done, and leave you to apply your own particular images. In fact, many of the designs that I will use in this book are best described as "whimsical". They are there just to give quick, easy, recognizable ideas about how you really can use just about any image to make a Tree that is relevant to you and your family. Still, you may like to copy one of these designs, for your personal use, or you might find that one might please a child, and you can get him/her hooked on the genealogy bug at a young age.

Not an artist ?

You can get images from many different sources, much as a scrapbooker does, that might include clip-art books and cds, stencils, stickers, magazines, photos, and more. These are readily and cheaply available from scrapbook shops, artist and hobby shops, school supplies, and even the big chains such as Wal-Mart have some. Have a look around. We are surrounded by visual stuff, much of it useful for a Tree. Clip-art and stickers, in particular, often come in sets and themes that range from old military vehicles to fashions to animals to cartoon characters to dinosaurs to tools to nature to stars to farms to patterns to ships to religion, and on and on. I can only suggest that you go and browse.

Notice Copyright Notice.

The only thing to watch is the copyright. You might use a picture from a magazine, which is okay if you hang the Tree on your wall….that's no worse than the pictures of pop stars that we all stuck up at one time….but please note that you can't then copy your Tree (for a sister perhaps) as that would then be an infringement. However, much of the stuff is copyright-free, you just need to be aware of what is and what isn't.

Copy, copy, copy.

Copying a Tree is a good idea though. Once you have gathered the information together, and displayed in on an attractive Tree, the next thing to consider is how to preserve it all. You can use acid-free paper, ink, framing and storage materials, of course, but you can also greatly increase survivability by doing copies. Send one to a family member, your local genealogical society, or one in a town where your ancestors lived. This way you may avoid a disaster, and I have heard several sad stories of floods, fires and hurricanes. The same applies to photos, certificates, stories, etc.

You could even do up some sort of package of the Tree, some photos, certificates, and the juiciest stories (including your own), and add it to a family member's Birthday or Christmas present. This would work as an introduction into the family history for a youngster……I remember visiting, as a tot, several great aunts and uncles. However, they were long gone before I understood that they were grandad's brothers and sisters. Cousins share half of your grandparents, so you can compare similarities and differences that might have been inherited. They may even have different memories, for example my mother's mother lived for many years, after she was widowed, with my aunt and cousins. I remember gran as a tall, slim, gracious lady, but my cousins tell me that she enjoyed watching wrestling on t.v. ! Likewise, if you present a package to an aunt or grandmother, they will surely appreciate your work and the strength of your family feelings, but they may also be encouraged to add more to your information by way of photos, stories and descriptions of those on the Tree, including some who you may have never met. Facts such as birth dates can always be gleaned from the official records, but the memories go wherever people go when they die. This is why we call our website grillyourgranny, as a reminder to collect everything that you can, while you can. Sometimes tomorrow is too late.

We don't do Trees, and the family research, just for ourselves. However, there is the old saying about not knowing where you are going until you know where you've been. This applies to your roots, from which you derive a lot of your physical look, your character, cultural ideas, opinions, and so on. Genealogy helps you to learn who you are, and your place in some wider schemes. You are part of your family past and future (even if childless, you might be an uncle), as well as the age and place that you grew up in, and live in. The more that you understand yourself, the better you can go forward.

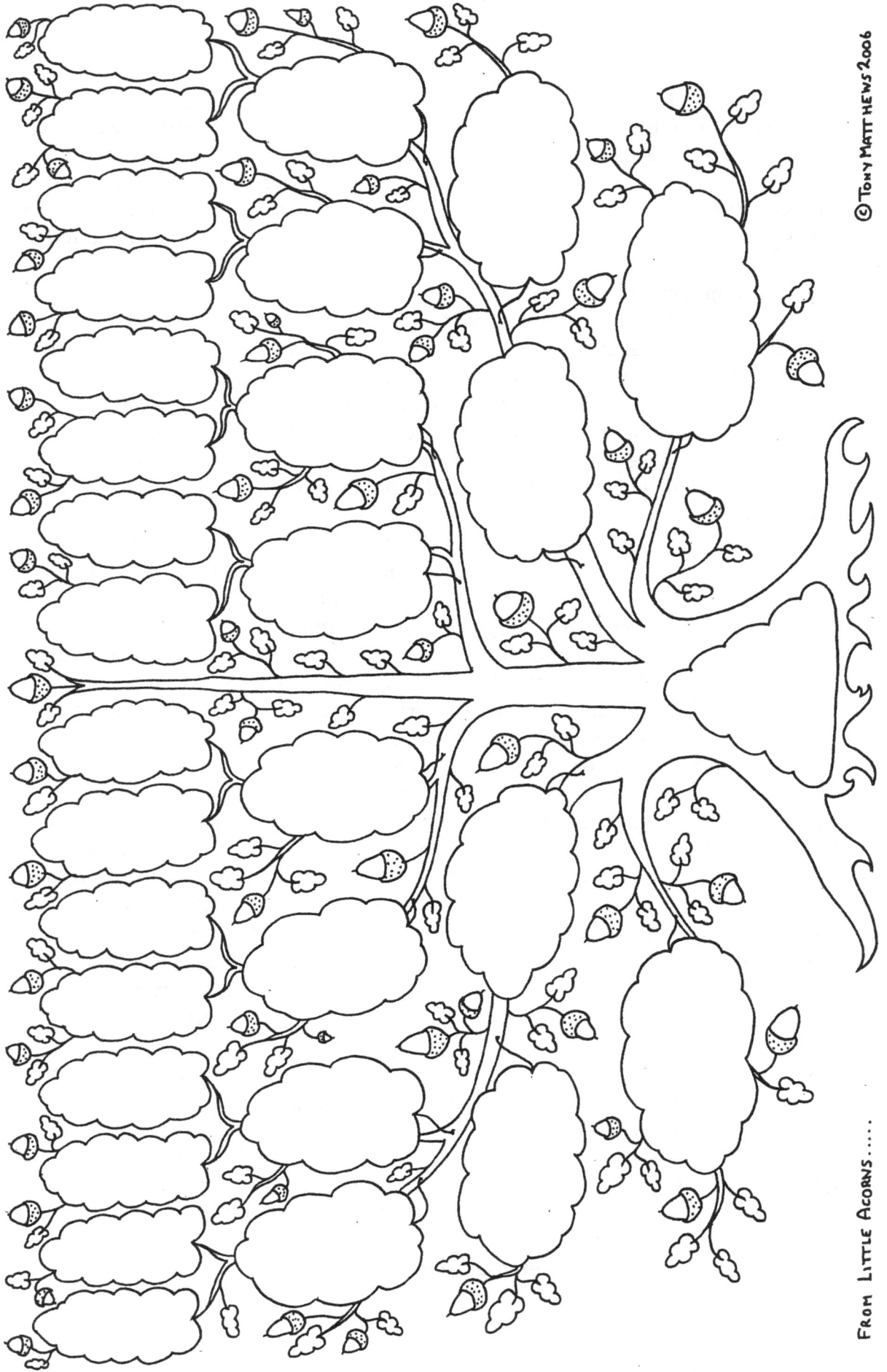

From Little Acorns......

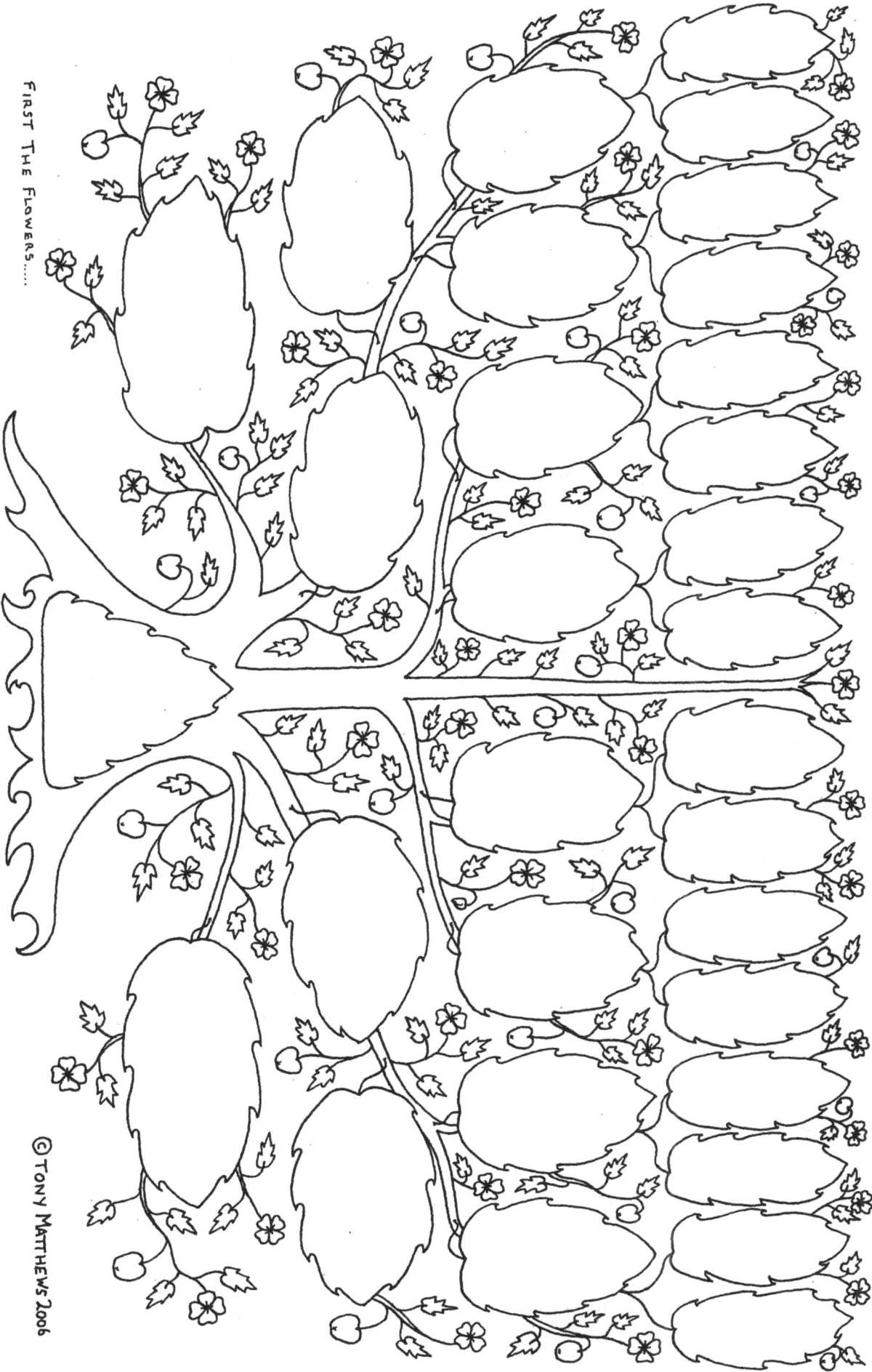

First the Flowers.....

© Tony Matthews 2006

HARVEST © Tony Matthews 2005

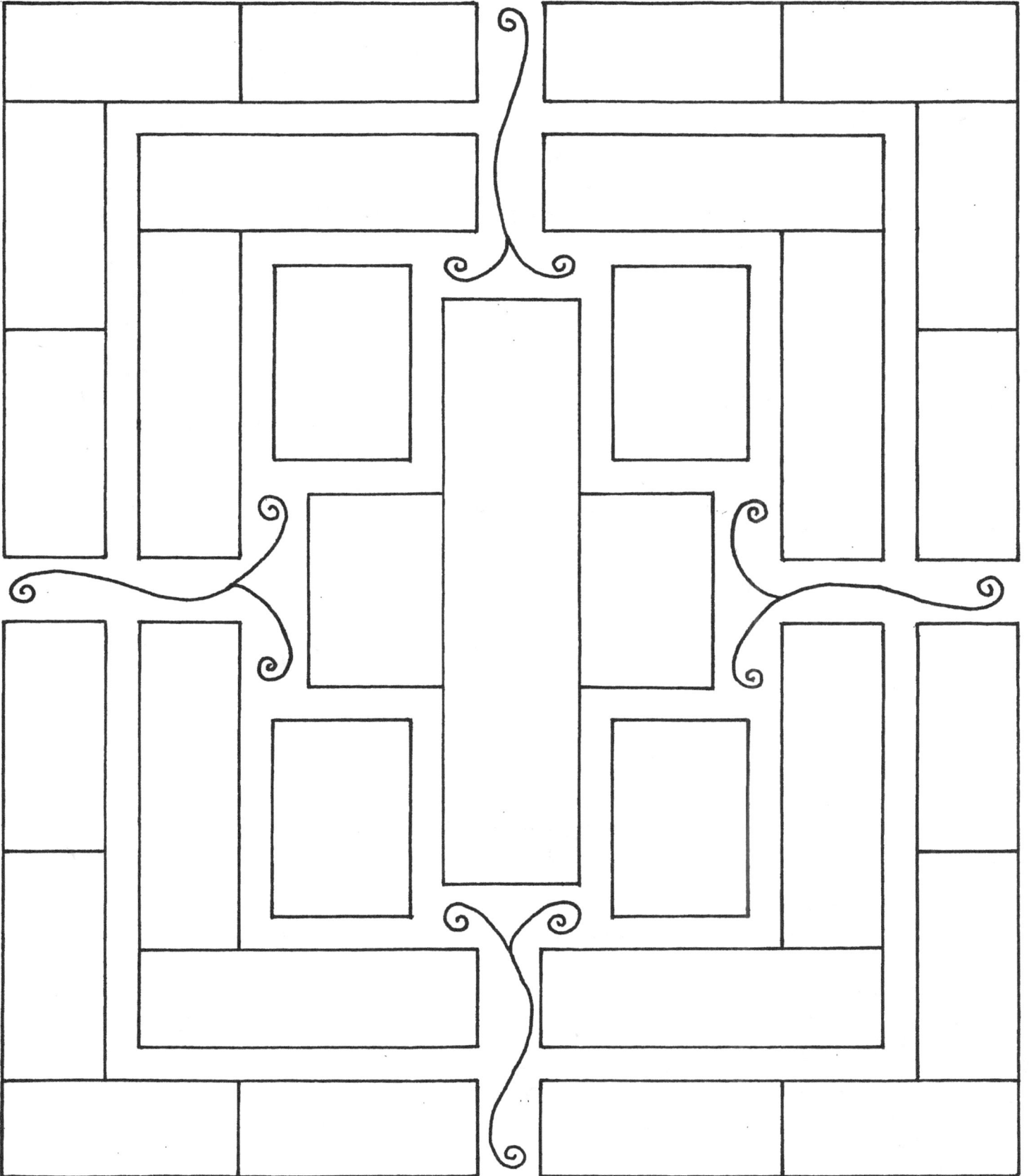

SIMPLICITREE

A Tree Or Not A Tree.

I mentioned the normal 1-2-4-8-16 format, which is not only called a Tree, but terms such as pedigree, lineage, kinship, bloodline, ancestry, etc. are also used to casually describe the same. We need to reconsider these terms, for you will find a special section later on in this book that is devoted to Trees that aren't really Trees at all in the usual sense. We might call them Family Histrees ?
What they are, are charts in, say, a 1-3-6-12-24 format, that are for certain special family situations. Some have been with us for a while, some are fairly recent, and some are still on the horizon.

The whole point is that some of these designs are not pedigree, not bloodlines, or only partially so. One simple example is for a child born of his/her natural mother and a sperm donor. Perhaps the husband is infertile due to some illness. However, he is the one that raises the child with his wife, the natural mother. What my designs includes is the whole history with the biological parents as well as the husband/guardian/caretaker, whatever we might call him, on it. Still, the child will think of him as "dad" and want him on the chart. However, the sperm donor is also important, even if he never even meets the couple and child, for it is his DNA that is passed on, his medical history that may have some bearing on the child's future welfare.....consider a hereditary disease.

Adopted folk have been with us forever, and I often hear statements, about filling in a Tree, such as " But half of it will be blank.". However, these people often have a spouse and children, so there is a Tree there, albeit the adopted person will be a short branch. What I've done is to come up with designs that are balanced, and will leave no blanks. You might use the 1-2-2-4-8-16 chart to show the child, mum and dad (who was adopted), mum's parents, their parents, and so on. If you are an adopted child you might want a 1-4-8-16 chart that shows you, then both your natural and adopted parents, then on to all of their parents, etc. The first chart is a pedigree, but the second is a Family Histree.

You will find other designs for egg donors, single mothers, and the only just futuristic ones such as for a clone. Again, not all are bloodlines, but rather a history. The most important thing to do is to clearly mark where you have a donor, an adoptee, or whatever. In fact I will use the same design for several different situations, and it's a simple lesson to work out which ones are pedigree, and which aren't.

Of course, the Tree won't be the only place where you have this information. The shoebox under the bed, or the teetering pile on the kitchen table, has this, and more....more facts on each person, plus all of the aunts, cousins, in-laws and other collateral lines. Still, not only is the Tree a simple visual, shows the main outlines of your pedigree, and makes an attractive wall hanging; but it is also the most likeliest thing to survive. Not every generation will have your fascination with their roots, but I think they would have to be very hard-hearted to discard your beautiful hand-made effort. Then one day their kids may come across it, and start asking questions.

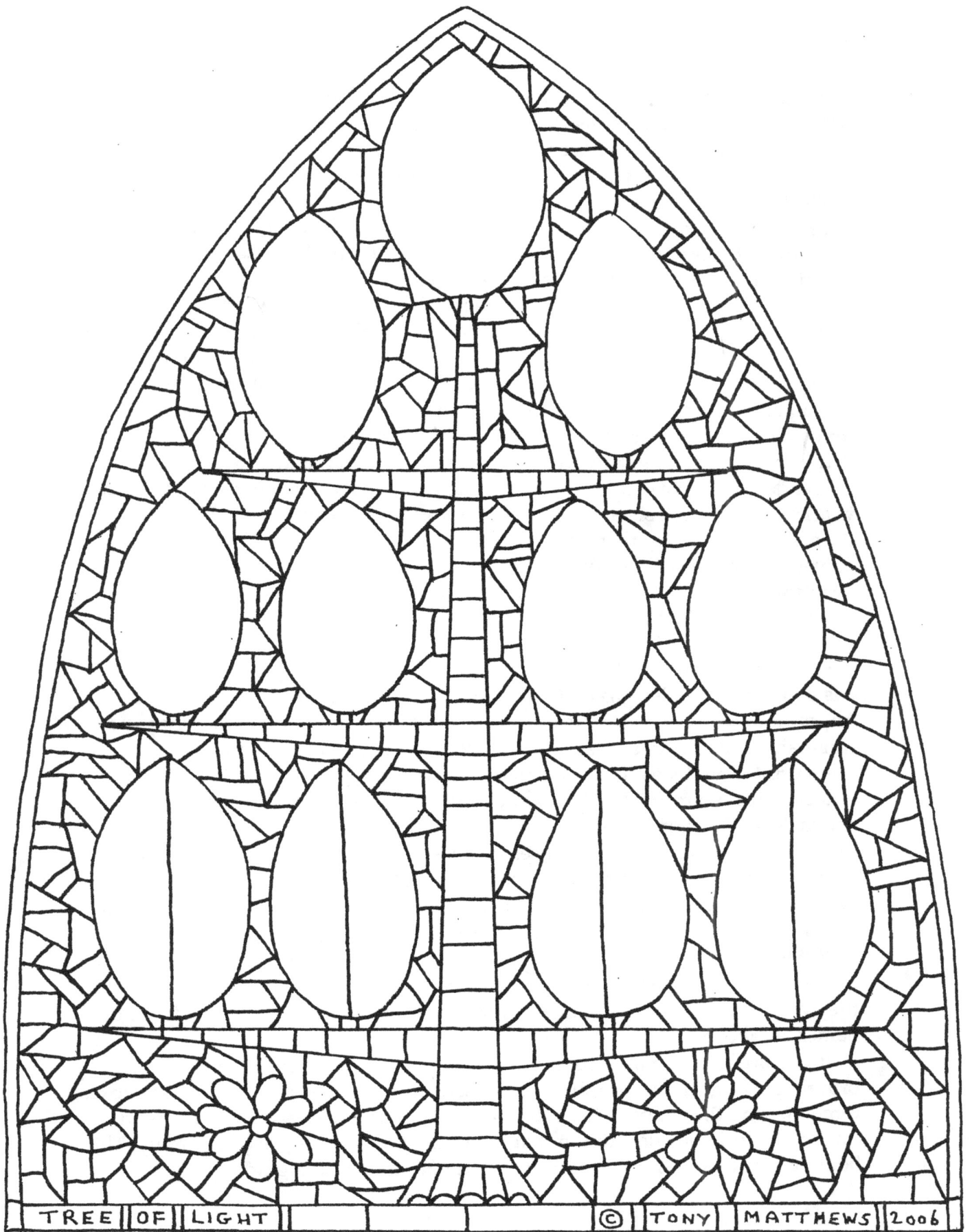

TREE OF LIGHT © TONY MATTHEWS 2006

Filling in.

Which brings us to the subject of how to fill in a Tree. I don't know how many times I've heard the faint-hearted excuse that "my handwriting's terrible". Yes, well, mine is too, but there are many ways around it which deserve some discussion, and which will encourage you to have a go.

The first thing to mention, though, is a simple scenario : you are clearing out a deceased grandparent's attic, and you come across a Tree that she drew up, all filled in with her spidery handwriting. Would you not clasp that to your bosom, and treasure it as a family heirloom ? I think that we can all agree on that.

So, consider at least having a try. Practice by drawing a few boxes on a scrap of paper, then write in some names, using a pencil lightly to see how it looks. Perhaps you could print the names, such as you learnt to do at school. Above all, take your time. When your pencil version looks halfway reasonable…ink over it. Use a pen with acid-free ink, they are cheap and readily available, and will last much longer. Later you can erase any pencil marks that still show.

If you still haven't got an acceptable result….and remember that your descendants will treasure it anyway….then we can look at other ways of filling in a Tree. Does your sister have better handwriting ? Your cousin ? Your kid ? It's always interesting to get other family members involved. You could of course, budget allowing, have a professional calligrapher do it for you, and get a beautiful result that way. But there are still other alternatives, some technical, others requiring handcraft.

One easy way.

For example, here at Papertree, we have on our grillyourgranny website some cds that have Tree designs on them. They are simple tif images that you can import into many art/graphic programmes on your computer. Once there you can manipulate the image, and type in your names, choosing a font that you like. Then print it off. Okay, most of you only have the regular letter size printer, but you can burn your finished Tree onto a cd, then take it to a whole range of copy shops, Kinko's, banner makers etc., who can print it out for you, as big as is possible. There are many other uses for these images too, for there are kits available so that you can show off your finished Tree on a mug, mouse pad, tote bag, or t-shirt. Then they make good additions in your files, showing the main line in each file, and likewise they can come into play at family reunions.

But what if you have a Tree that you have designed yourself ? Good for you, now you just have one extra step to do. Take it to that same banner maker, and they will be able to scan it onto a cd for you. Take it home, and start adding the names, as above.

If you are really smart you might design the whole thing on your computer by bringing up a grid, like graph paper, onscreen. Then you can work out the boxes, remembering the simple 1-2-4-8-16 format. Next you use, say, a cd of clip-art images, to add your decoration that it pertinent to you and/or your family. This book has many different designs in it that you can use as a guide.

Even less technical.

Still, not everyone, is very computer savvy…..including me…..so what can you do ? Start with your own design, or even one printed at the banner maker from one of our cds, or one of the blanks copied from this book. To add the names you go back to your school days. You, or someone can do it for you, simply type out the names on a computer, word processor, or typewriter. Then get out the scissors and glue stick. Cut out the names, glue them in place, et voila, you have you a Tree with legible names.

You can take it one step further and make a copy that won't have bits of paper hanging on it. Many copy shops and banner makers have a big machine for copying maps and blueprints, although mostly in black and white. Still, they could scan your Tree, if you want colours and have used copyright-free material, and then do you a print out.

My best suggestion.

Then you could use the method that gives you the best of both worlds. You do your Tree, and fill in the names yourself as best as you can. But you are still worried that although your descendants will love it, they might not be able to read all of the names. Okay, here's what you do. As you fill in each name you number the box (details below), then on a sheet of paper type out those numbers and corresponding names. Slip that sheet into an acid-free page protector which you glue to the back of your framed Tree, or in some way keep the sheet and Tree together. Now you have both a handwritten Tree, and the facts clearly typed. The best of both worlds.

As for the numbering system, the traditional one is simplest. You, or the subject of the Tree, are number one. Men, traditionally, go to the left, or above, according to the design, so that dad is 2 and mum 3. It then follows on naturally that dad's dad is 4, dad's mum is 5, mum's dad is 6, and mum's mum is 7. Continue like this for as many generations as you like. A curious fact emerges that the father is always twice the child, and mother follows diligently after. Thus the father of number 17 will be 34, and the mother 35. That's the traditional system, but as long as your number is clearly marked you can do it any way that you like.

Any more excuses ? Well, I suppose you could give this book to a daughter or a brother, and offer your services as a technical advisor. Otherwise, we have a design called Hope that we can customize not only to include your parents, grandparents and great grandparents, but also your children, and even grandchildren. We can add the names for you, and send you the results on a cd, ready to go to the copyshop.

In the near future we hope to have our big printer up and working, and will then be able to print the Tree for you, up to 22X17. There is a charge, of course, but why are we doing Trees in the first place ?

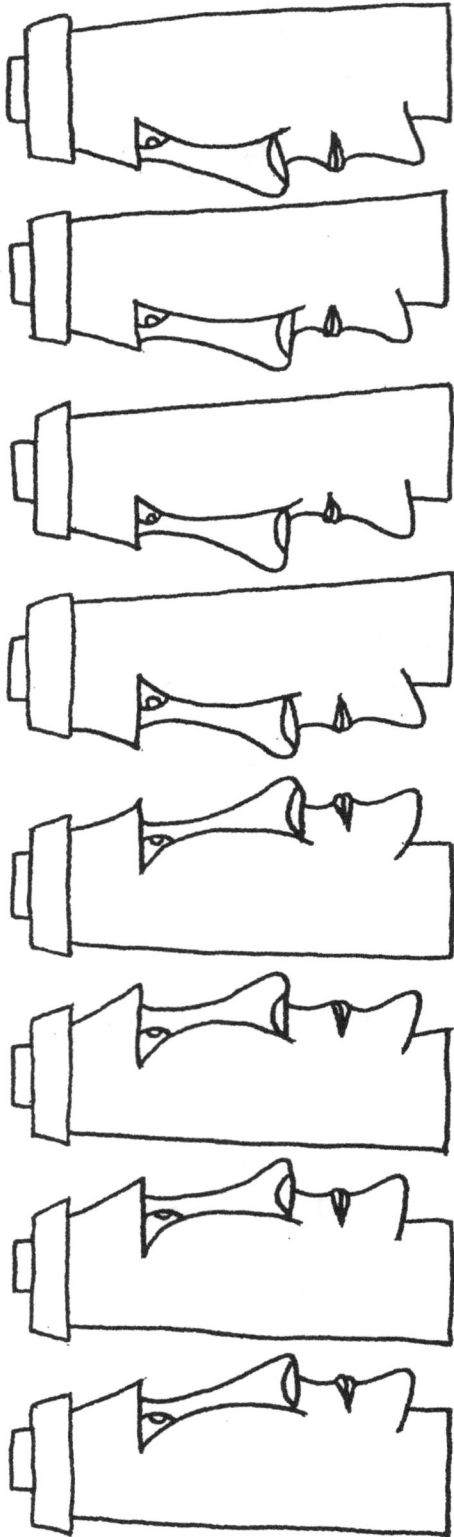

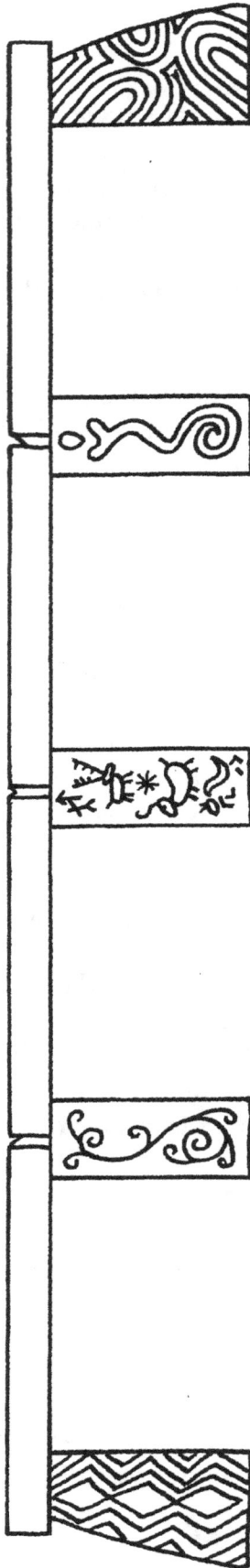

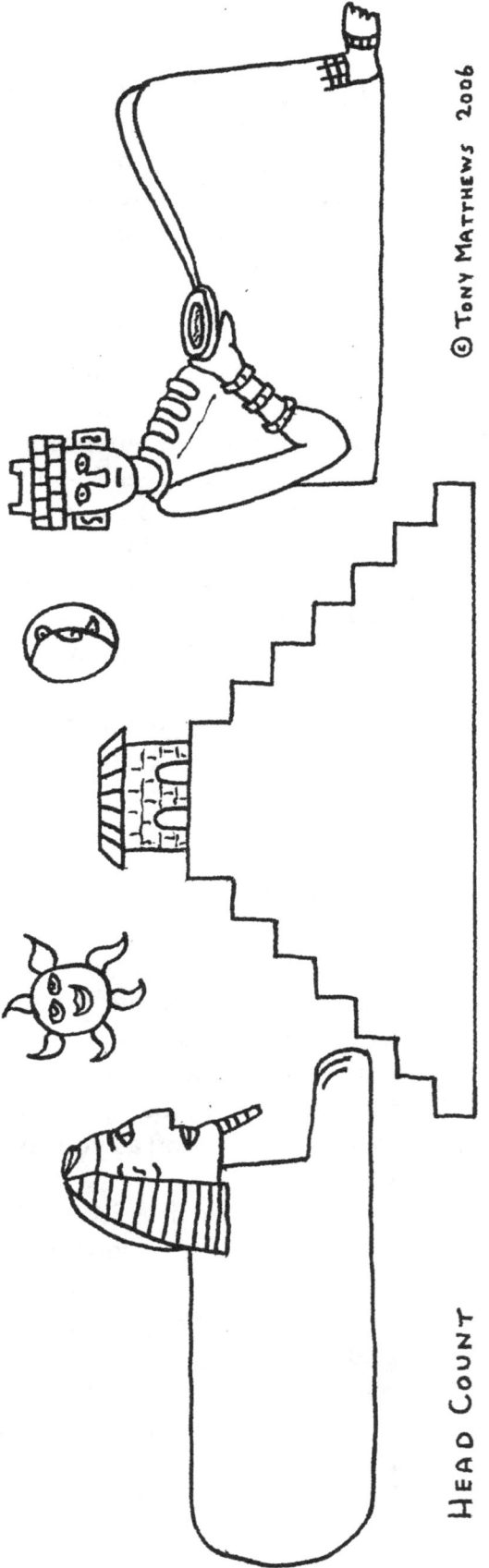

© Tony Matthews 2006

Head Count

TONY'S
HEAD COUNT

© Tony Matthews 2006

JOSEPH MATTHEWS
17 May 1849 Bracknell
Ag.lab.+ Broom Maker

ANNIE RICHARDSON
20 Jan 1850
(m) 31 March 1872 Bracknell

CHARLES HENRY LANE
bp. 18 July 1841
Marylebone, London

MARY ?
Marylebone, London.

WILLIAM COOKE

HENRIETTA YOUNG

WALTER KEEBLE
Brockham, Suffolk
10 Jan 1862

JEMIMA LOUISA LUCAS
1854 Ramsey, Essex
(m) 17 Oct 1888 Tendring
Reg. off. Essex

EDWARD WALTER
MATTHEWS
5 April 1872
Bracknell,
Berks, England.
BRICKLAYER

LOUISA MATILDA
LANE
21 June 1880
WILLESDEN,
LONDON
(m) 6 Ap 1901 Bracknell

ERNEST
COOKE
1885
Battersea/Wandsworth.
+ small garage, piano
mover, ambulance driver

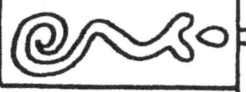

HILDA MAUD LUCAS
KEEBLE
19 Nov 1884
Black Boy Pub,
Westley, Essex
(m) 2 April 1921
Ramsey, Essex

GEORGE
MATTHEWS
5 Aug 1920
Bullbrook, Bracknell
Carpenter. Piano Accordian Player

ANTHONY
RAYMOND
MATTHEWS
7 May 1949 Bracknell, Berks
(m) Linda Goetsch 17 Jan 1984 Grand Canyon
Family Tree Designer, writer and poet,
gardener, astrologer, cartoonist, traveller.

JOYCE
MARGERY
COOKE
11 April 1922
Cholsham, Surrey
(m) 10 May 1944
Warfield, Berks

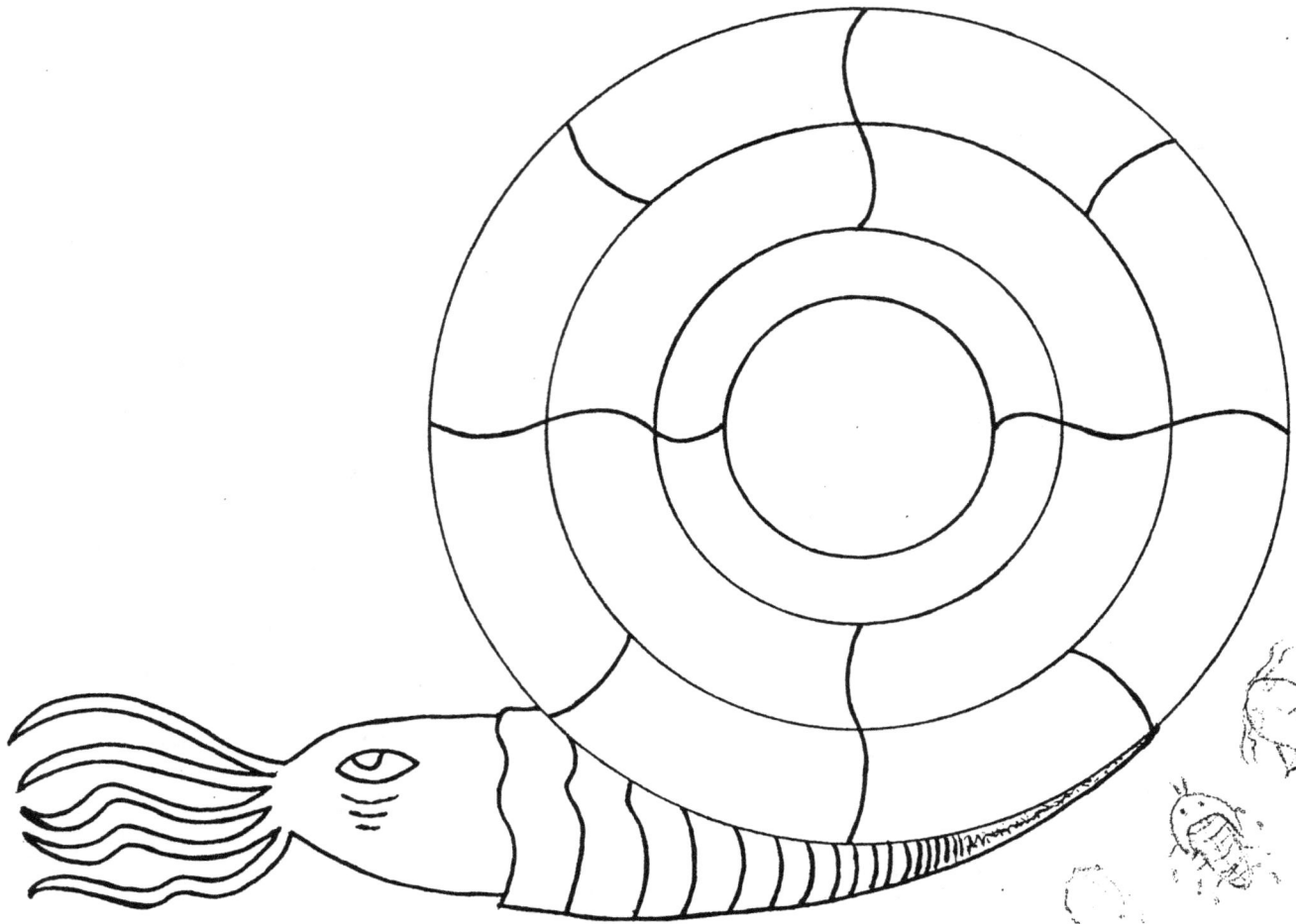

A NAUGHTY LASS!

2004 ©TONY MATTHEWS

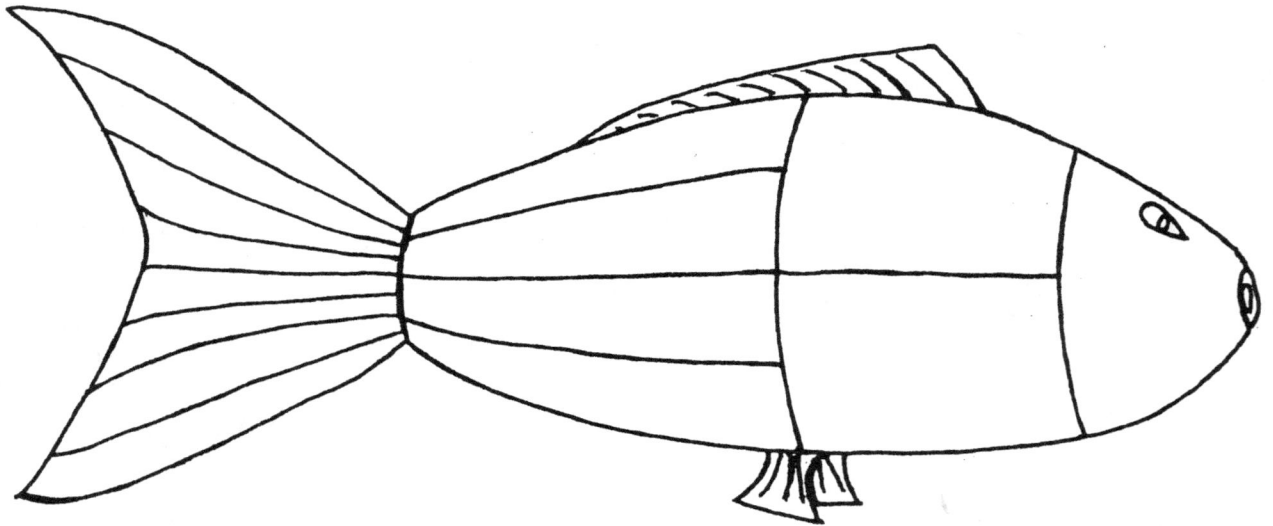

DROP ME A LINE?

©TONY MATTHEWS 2004

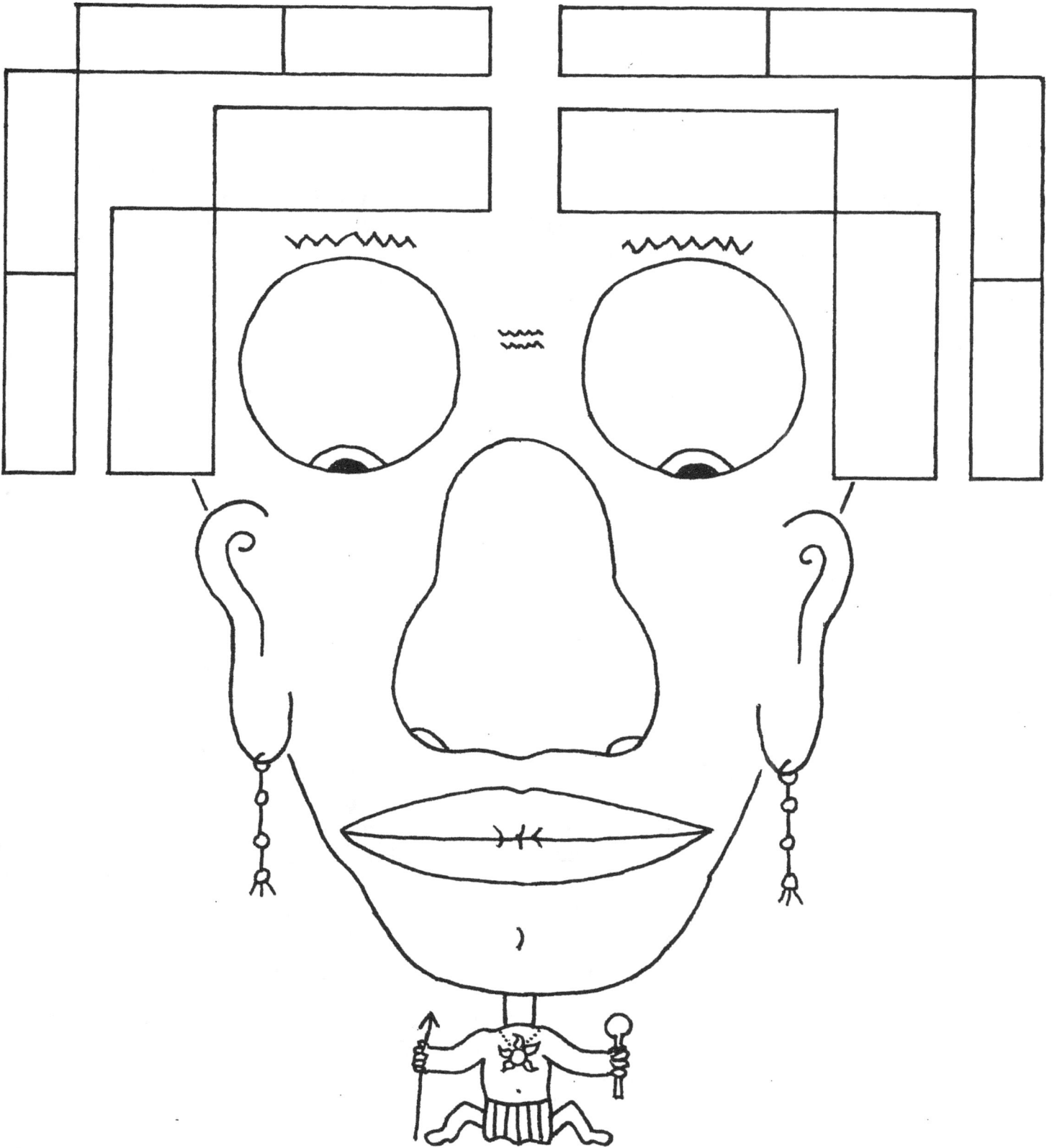

BIG ED (IDOLATREE)

© TONY MATTHEWS 2006

It's OK To Be A Show-off.

There are 2 levels to this. Firstly, you have done a lot of hard work (and had a lot of fun probably) in doing the research, and want to proudly show off the results, and quite rightly so. That beautiful framed Tree hanging on your wall will be praised, and be a wonderful conversation piece. The second, and possibly more important reason, is the preservation of your family history. Granted the Tree only shows your pedigree/bloodline, and doesn't include all of your information on these ancestors, nor does it include all of the cousins, uncles, in-laws, etc. What it does preserve is what I call the skeleton of your family. If all of your notes in the shoebox under the bed are cruelly tossed out by your children, they may well at least hang on to your beautiful Tree....and future generations will have a huge start in their research. Or if you have sent your sister a copy, then her children might be interested in finding out more. Imagine if your mum had left you, say, a 6 generation Tree.....how much easier your research would have been.

This is particularly so if you include just a few pieces of information on each person. Date and place of birth are the prime facts, followed by date and place of marriage. If there is room, then the date and place of death is another useful piece of information. I like to include, where possible, a word or two of description such as farmer, carpenter, accountant, etc., that gives you a glimpse of the person. You might use something like football fan, stamp collector, classical music buff, practical joker, artist, or anything that you remember someone for. And ask yourself : what would you like to be remembered for ? Put that on your Tree too.

Be yourself.

We are not looking for perfection when it comes to a Family Tree. It is an expression of yourself, your knowledge and feelings about your family. The facts need to be straight, of course, but the decorations are truly open to whatever you want or are. Whether you are technically minded, a romantic, fantasist, have a silly humour, are practical, lazy, nature lover.....let it come out on the Tree. You are part of the same history. Sure, you want to make a good impression, but also let it be a true impression. Of course, if you are a murderer, you might want to choose some other facet of your personality to concentrate on....or maybe not ? Instead of framing your Tree to display it, you might simply pin it to the wall with a butcher's knife. Perhaps that's too extreme, but I trust that you get the point (ouch !) that for once the whole family is under your control, and you can say whatever you want about them. Then wait for the feed-back. Seriously, history is not just about queens and presidents and generals, it is about everyone, from the greatest to the least. You are the recorder for your little corner of life.

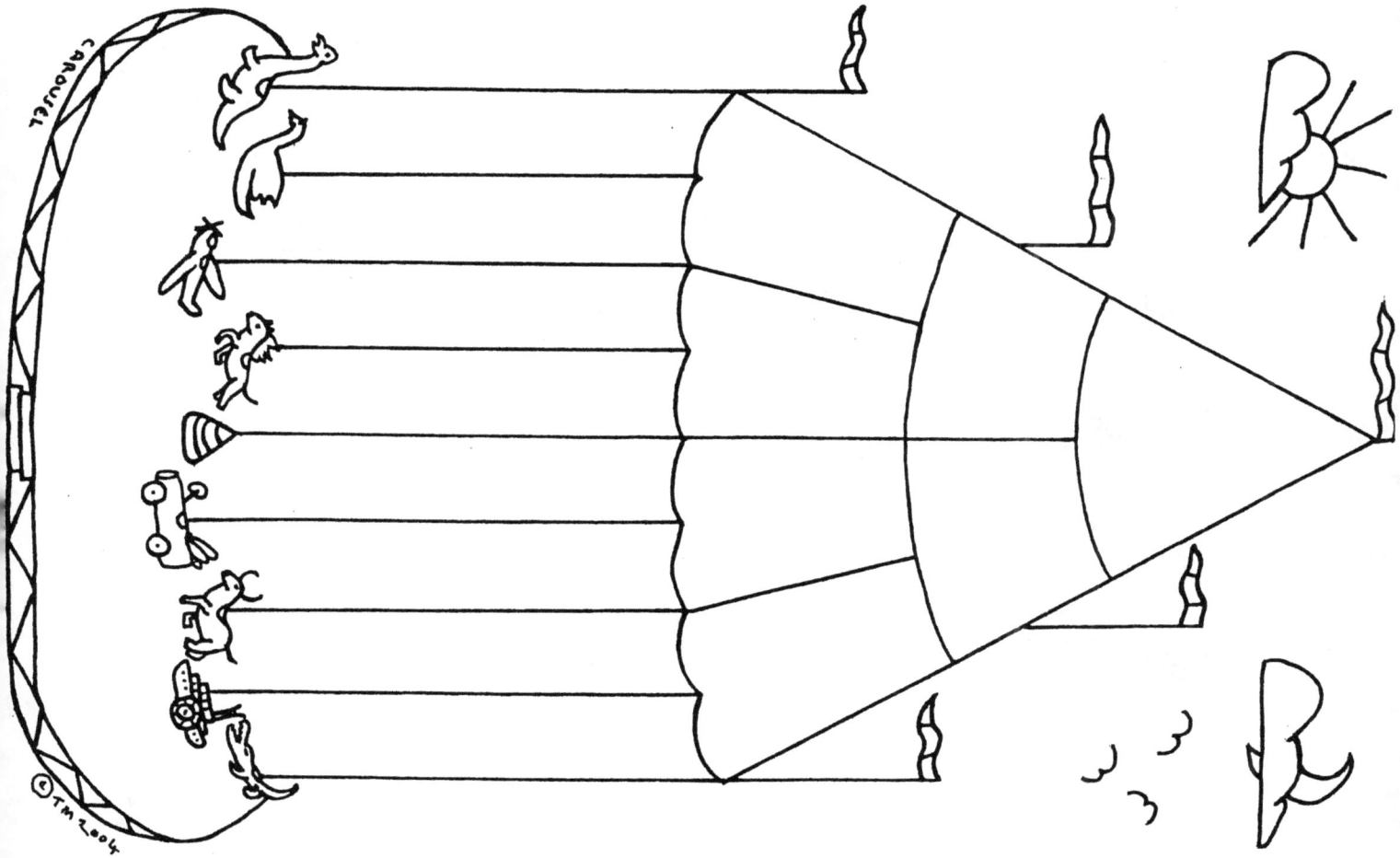

CAROUSEL

© TM 2004

GOOD VINTAGE

© Tony Matthews 2004

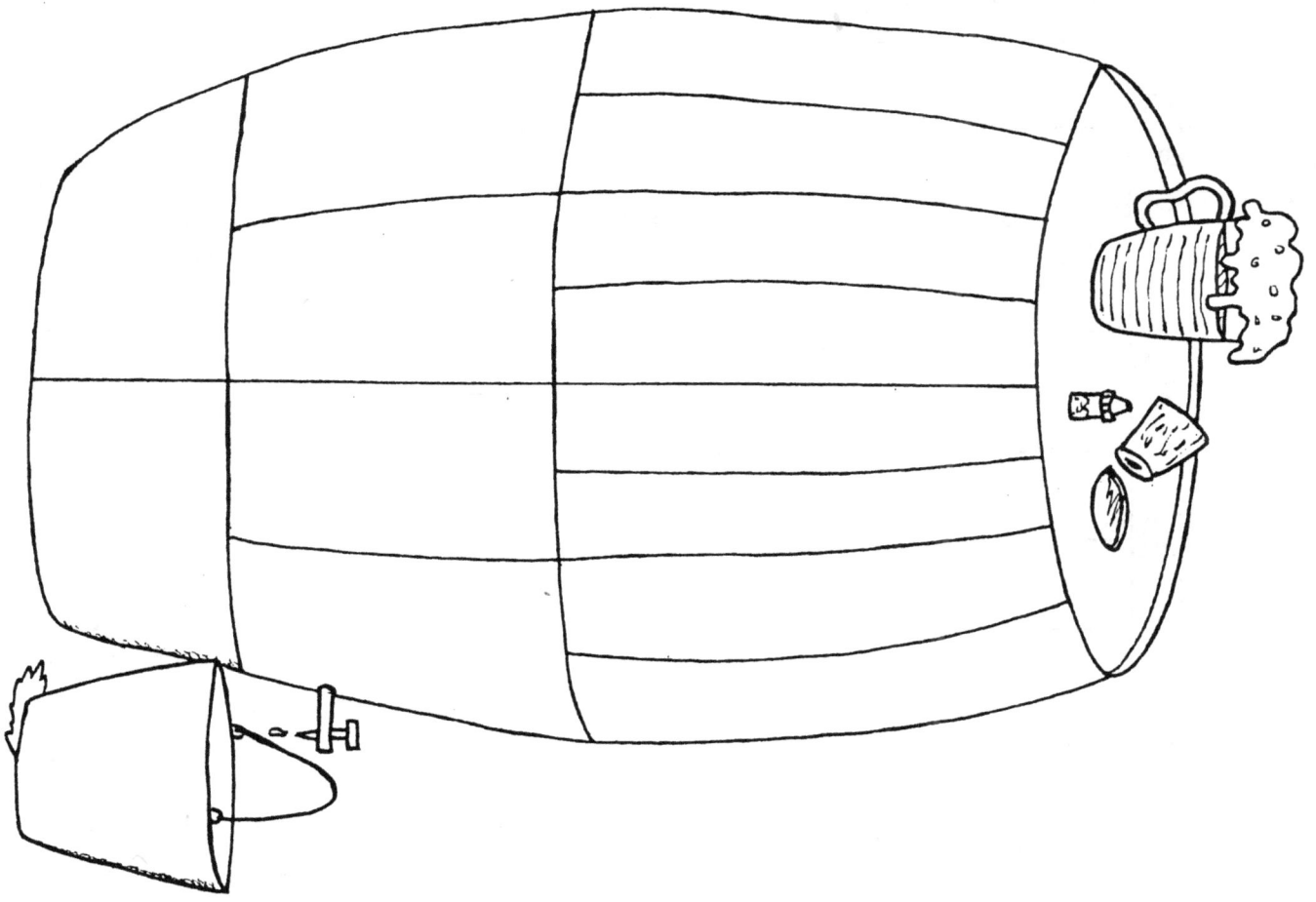

FAITH

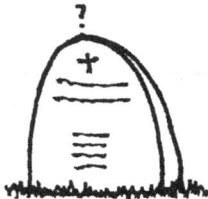

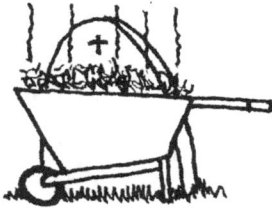

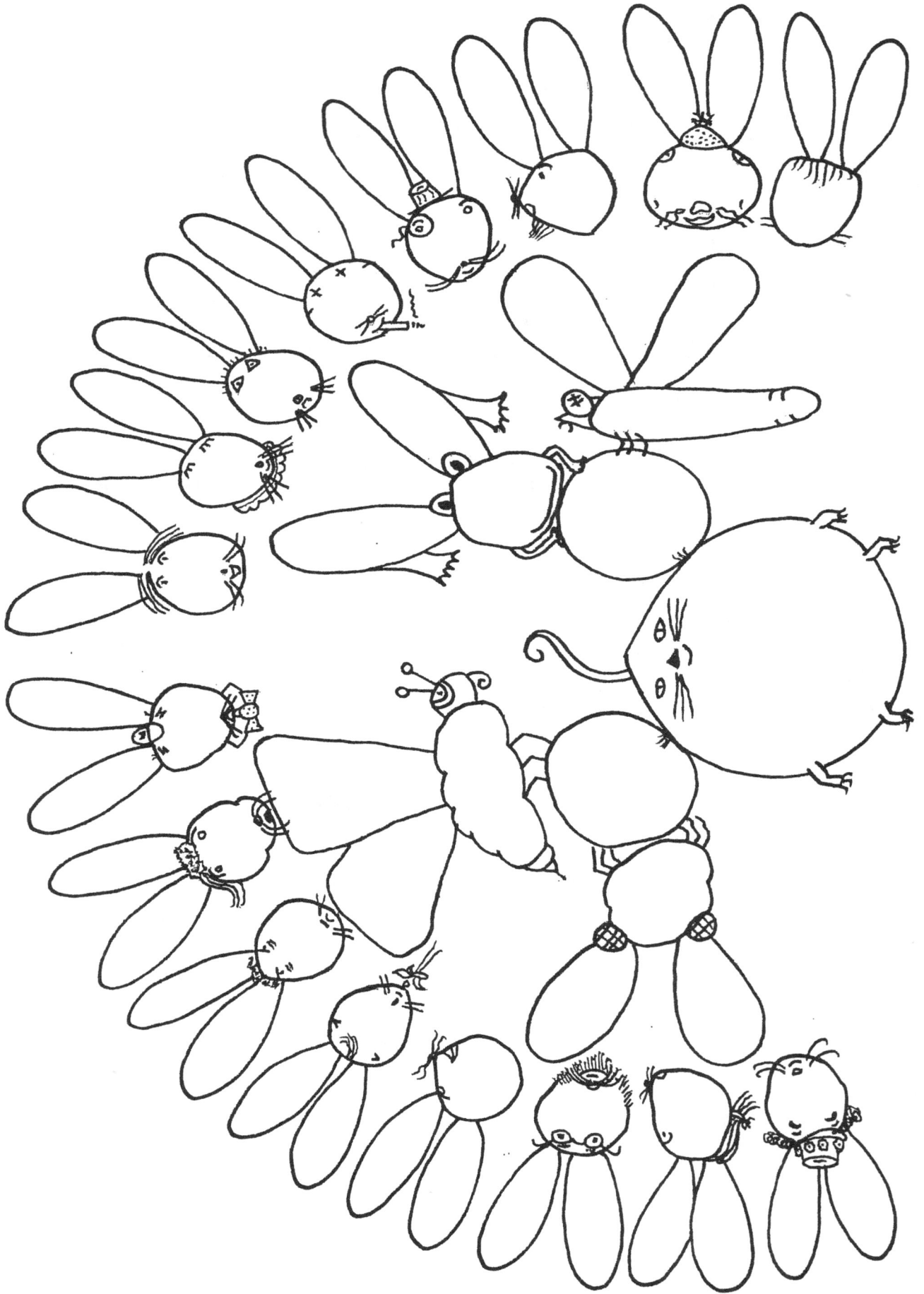

FAT MOUSE CHAIRS THE GENEALOGY MEETING

© TONY MATTHEWS 2006

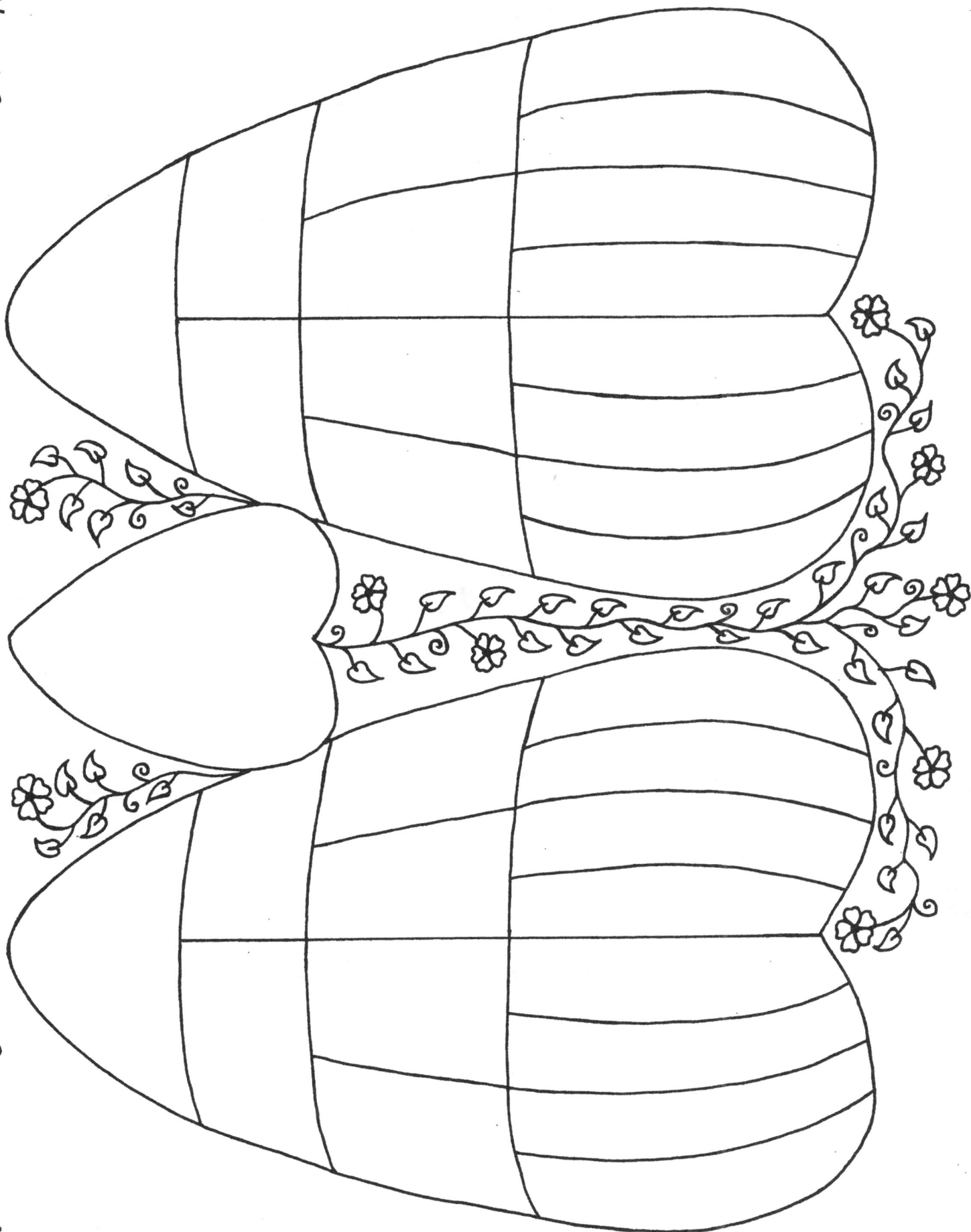

In Bloom

©Tony Matthews 2004

L. O. C. O.
Rail Road Co.

LOCO
FAMILY?

KEEP ON TRUCKIN'

2004 © Tony Matthews

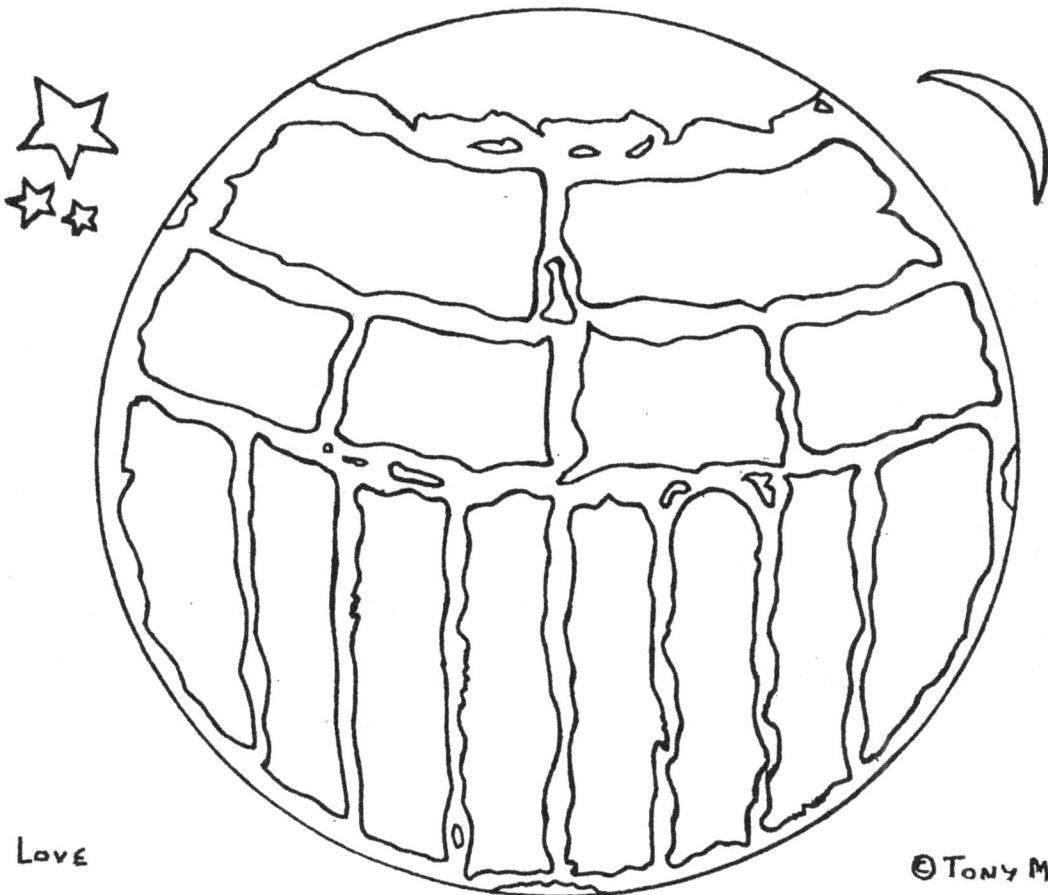

A World Of Love

© Tony Matthews 2004

Your turn.

On the next few pages you will find some blanks so that you can have a go. You might want to make a larger copy, and most copy shops will be able to shunt it up to 17X11. Some places will be able to go even bigger, and I like to use 17X22. You could also start from graph paper and do your own version, just by following my layout. Anyway, the idea is that you will be ready to add your images, as we've already talked about.

The very simplest one is called "**Your Pic**", and here you only need to add a single picture, on the square indicated, to personalize your Tree. That only leaves the filling in to do, as already discussed.

The next one, "**Your Frame**", goes a little further. Here there is a border, or frame, for you to fill with pertinent images. Kids might like this one too….do a copy and get them to choose a packet of stickers, then let them loose on it. You could help them putting in the names, teaching them a little family history as you do it. The thing is, having been involved in creating the Tree, they are more likely to want to hang on to it, and you will have the satisfaction of having passed your knowledge on.

If you are a little creative, you might want to try "**Your Shape**". It does take a little more imagination to think of an appropriate image for you or your family that will fit in here. Still, I ran off several copies for myself, sat and stared for a while, and in the following pages you will find a whole bunch of fairly quick and easy ideas that I came up with. Where I have a ship, you might think an antique car would express your ideal hobby better. My leaf could be your heart, star, or any other suitable shape. Oh, yes, and one or two of the designs are just me being cute, but I hope that they demonstrate the wide range of things that could work. I have also included one to show how the names would be traditionally organized.

To complete the quartet, there's "**Your Path**". It's a familiar layout, except that I have used less generations, but opened up the spaces between the boxes somewhat. This is so that instead of going around the outside, as in "Your Frame", here you can let your images wander amongst the boxes.

You might try a larger piece of paper, and lightly draw some boxes in this style. Next add your images, not worrying if you go slightly over your lines. Then fill in the names, and finally erase any remaining guide lines. This will give you a more open feel to the whole design. Not every family is regimented, and comfortable being in a box, but prefer to be spread out amongst beautiful or familiar things.

Remember that you can use the same format, but start from the top, or even left or right. Or if you copied my layout, then did a flipped version and put it below the original, with an additional box in the middle between them, then you will have the hourglass style. Similarly you could use an extra box in the middle, then do the original layout going left, and a flip going right. Then there's 3D…..

Your Pic

Your Pic

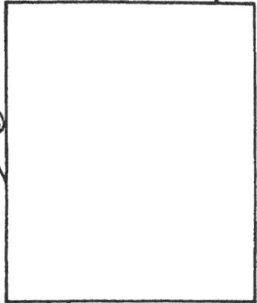
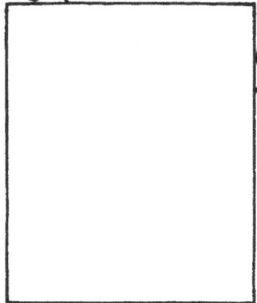
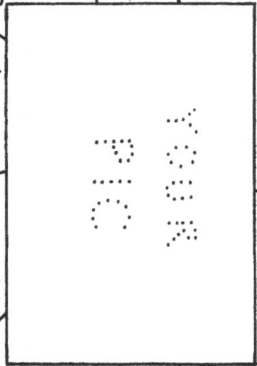
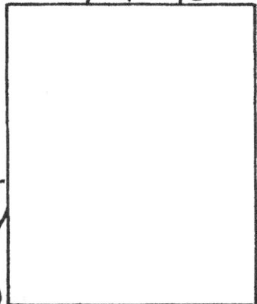

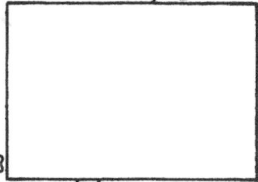

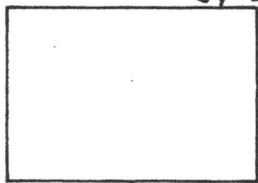
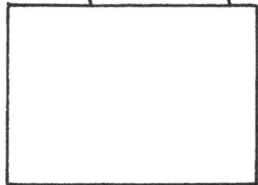
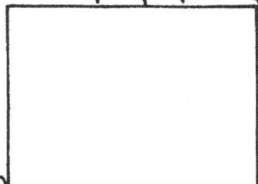

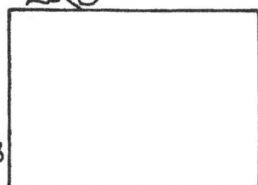

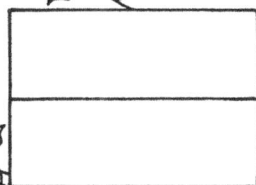

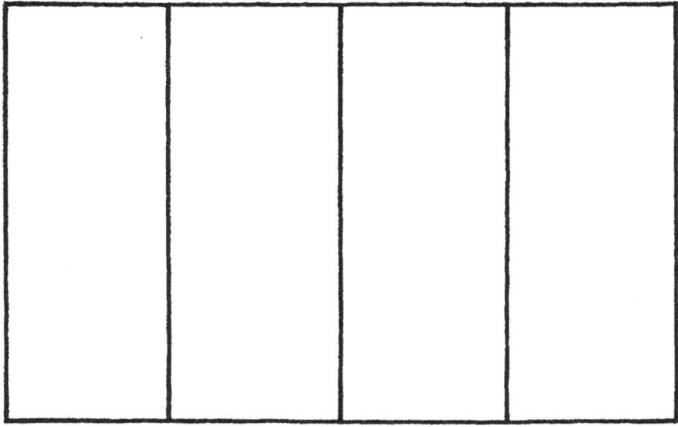

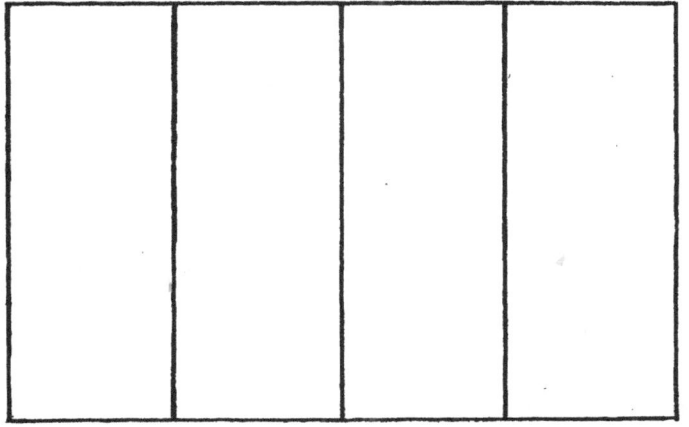

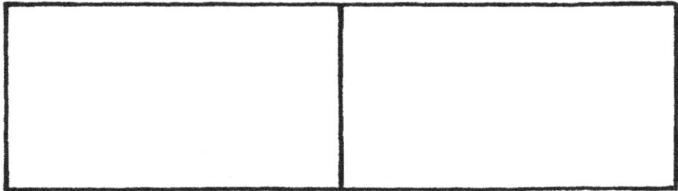

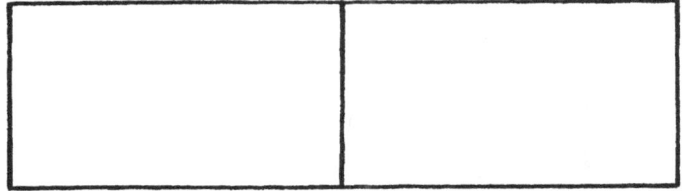

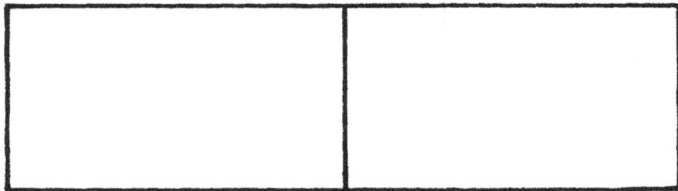

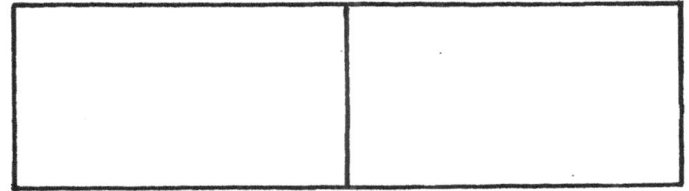

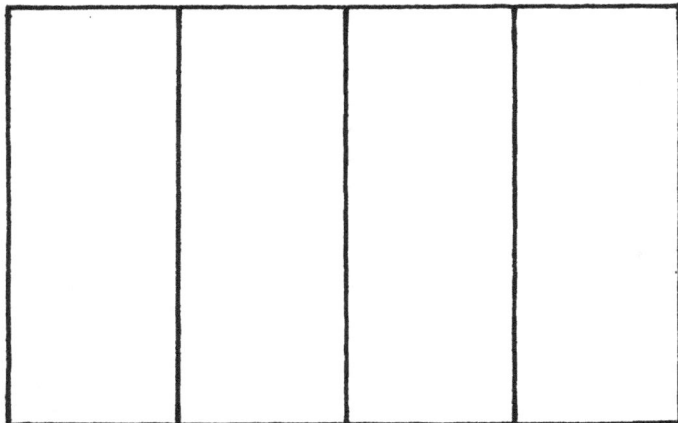

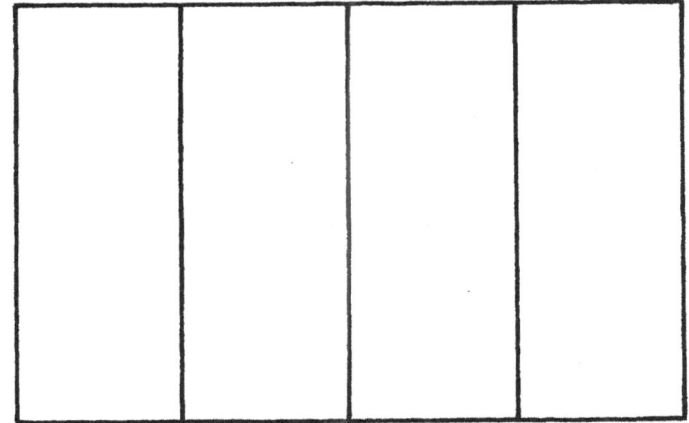

Your Path

D D D D	D D D M	D D M D	D D M M

M D D D	M D D M	M D M D	M D M M

DAD'S DAD'S DAD	DAD'S DAD'S MUM

MUM'S DAD'S DAD	MUM'S DAD'S MUM

DAD'S DAD

MUM'S DAD

DAD

SELF

MUM

DAD'S MUM

MUM'S MUM

D M D	D M M

M M D	M M M

D M D D	D M D M	D M M D	D M M M

M M D D	M M D M	M M M D	M M M M

LAY OUT

A

LIL' OAK

© TONY MATTHEWS 2006

ALL SOULS

NEW LEAF

© TONY MATTHEWS 2006

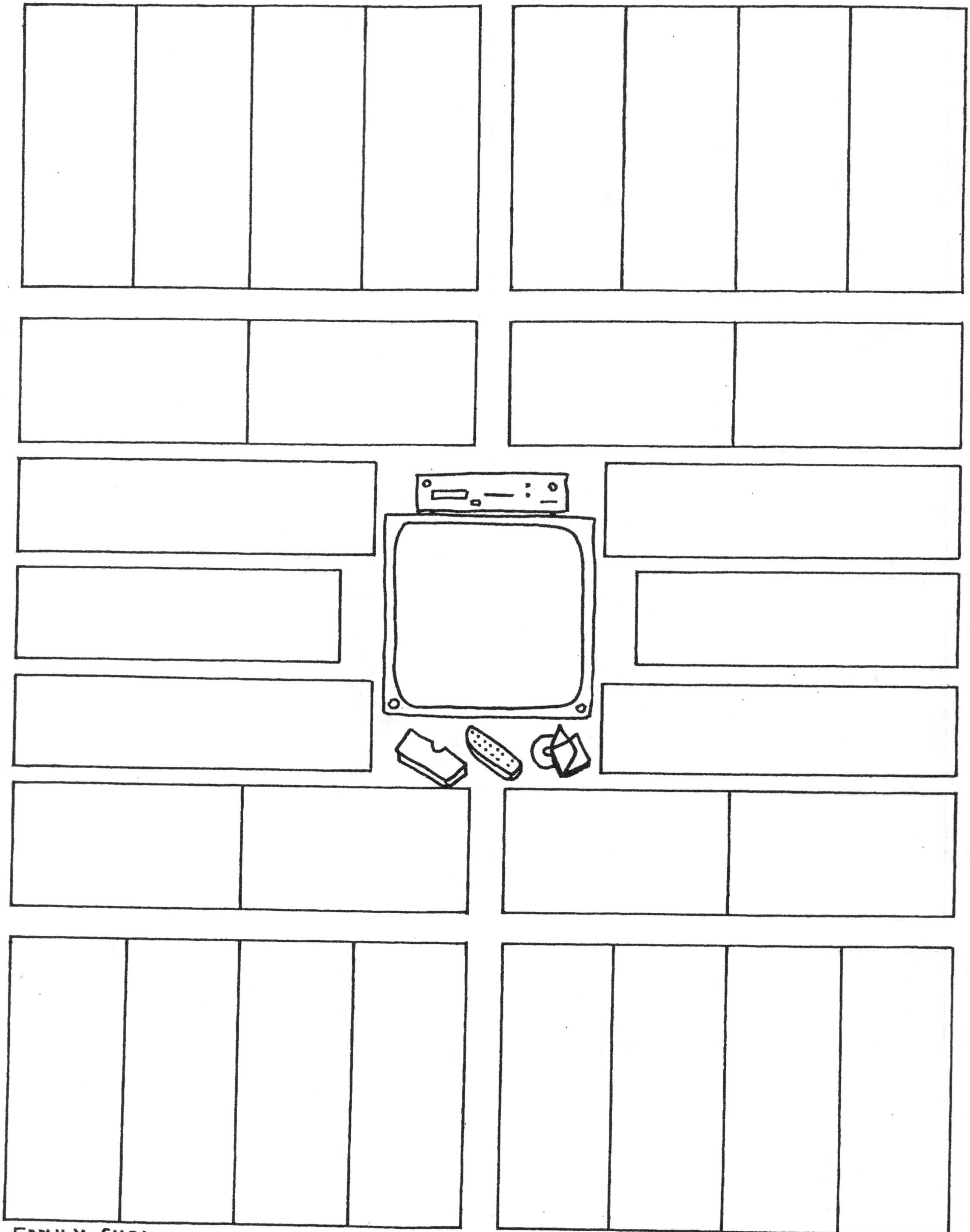

FAMILY SHOW

© TONY MATTHEWS 2006

TRILITHON

© TONY MATTHEWS 2006

SHIP-SHAPE

© TONY MATTHEWS 2006

SETTING

©TONY MATTHEWS 2006

SHARE WARE

© TONY MATTHEWS 2006

Ace

STEAMIN'

©TONY MATTHEWS 2006

FILL IN

ALL-STARS

©TONY MATTHEWS 2006

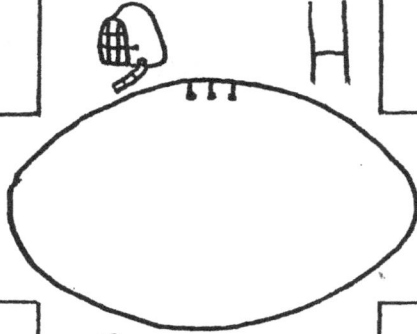

TEAM

© TONY MATTHEWS 2006

PAY ONE MILLION
$1,000,000
BONUS TO THE
BELOW NAMED:

Thanks Pal,
SIGNED: The Boss

CALIFORNIA DREAMIN'   © TONY MATTHEWS 2006

GENE POOL

A Work In Progress

STORY TIME

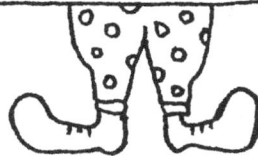

SHAPE UP

© TONY MATTHEWS 2006

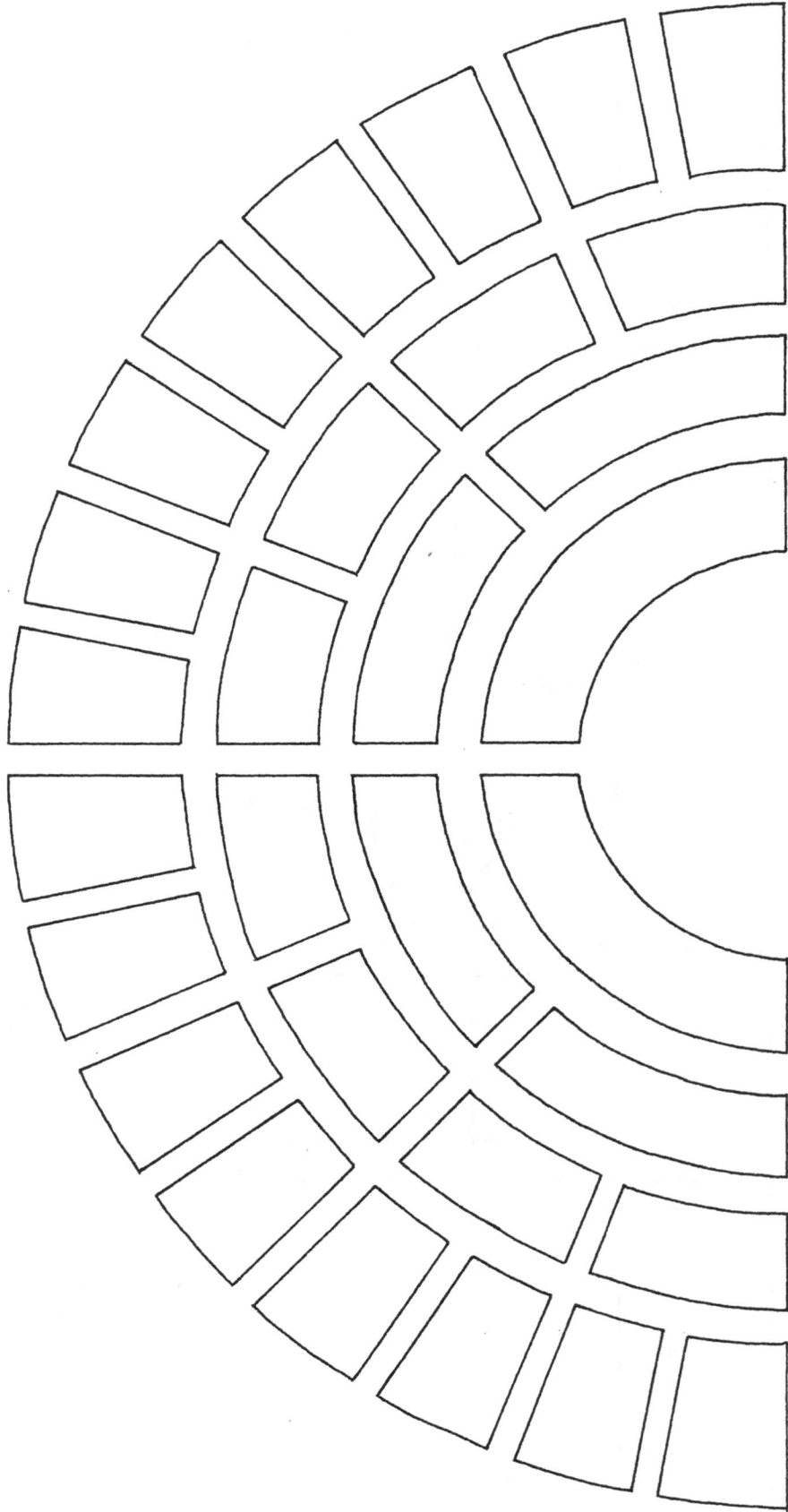

YOUR FAN

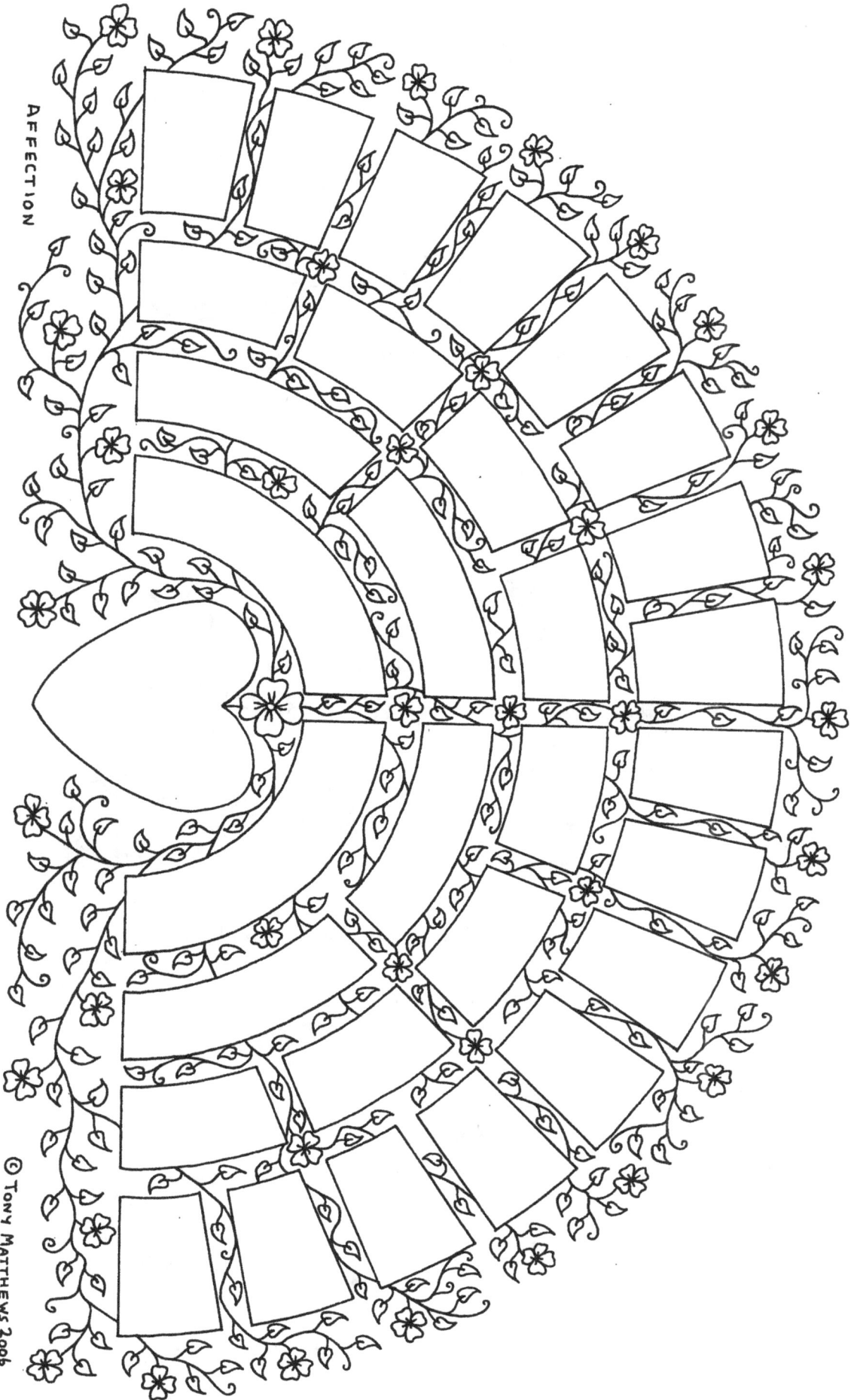

Even Diplodocus played hide 'n' seek.

Religion? No, just fermented apple juice.

Sometimes it's better to just walk away.

If it wasn't for the male *ego* we'd all be riding on those nice Eohippus by now.

WHAT !!! TEN YEARS GONE ALREADY ?

Rip Van Census Man.

OBSOLETE (Stonehenge).

It is cold out here,
On Salisbury Plain,
Waiting for a Master
To come here again.

The energy of the Earth
Thrums in our bones,
For we are the megalith,
Sarcens and trilithons.

Birth was a painful affair :
Hauled out of the ground,
Handled with little care,
Then pound, pound, pound,

Till we were in shape.
Then dragged and ferried,
And then pummeled again,
Before being half-buried.

We stand now in a circle,
And are carefully aligned.
That makes us so useful,
For the calculating mind.

They make their predictions,
They chant and they pray,
Well, for a few years....
Then they all went away.

Left us standing out here,
And one by one we fall,
And all you do is watch us,
But not use us at all.

So we wait for a Master,
To use those skills again.
Meanwhile it is cold here,
Out on Salisbury Plain.
****

© Tony Matthews 2006

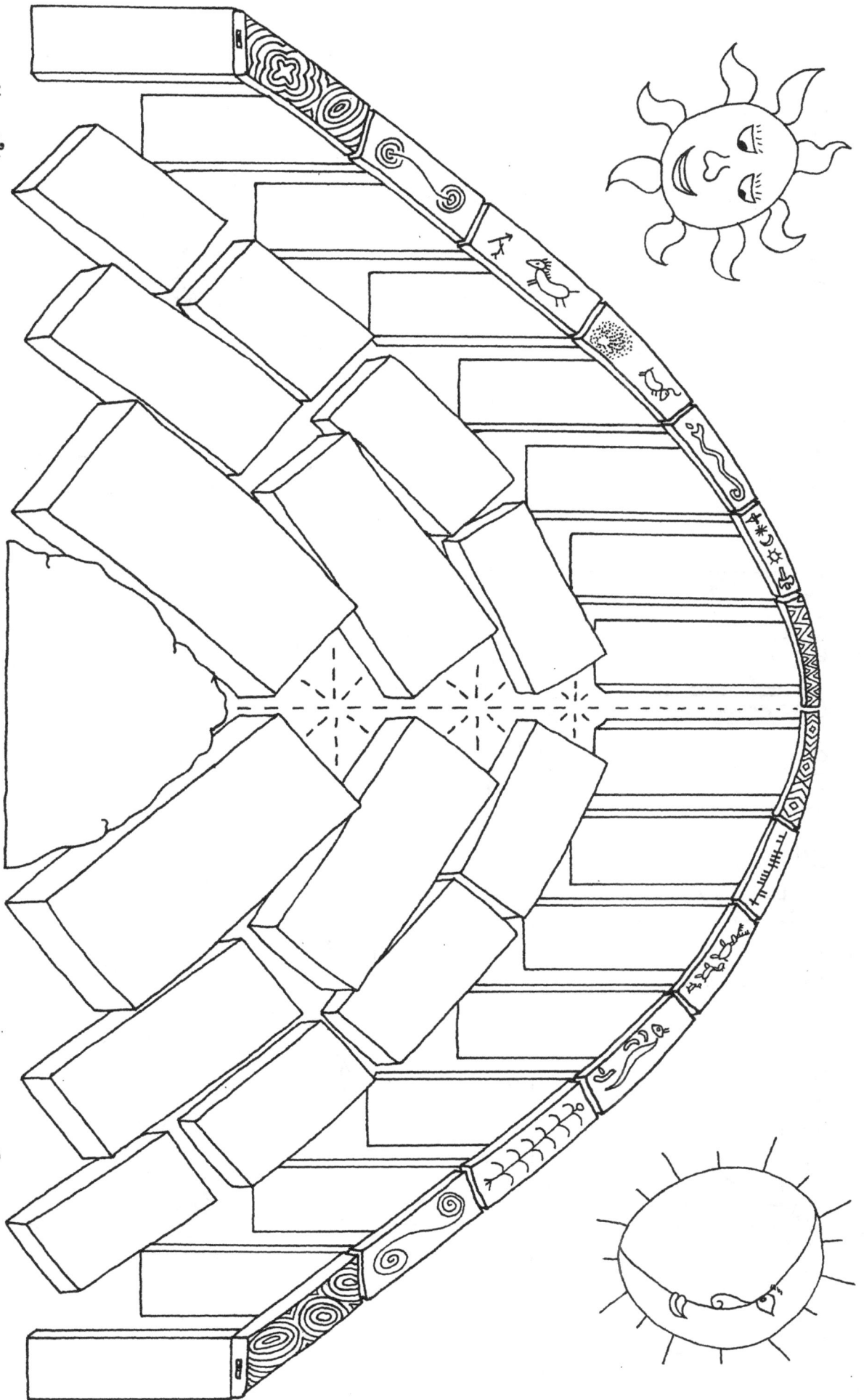

Meg A' Lith

© Tony Matthews 2006

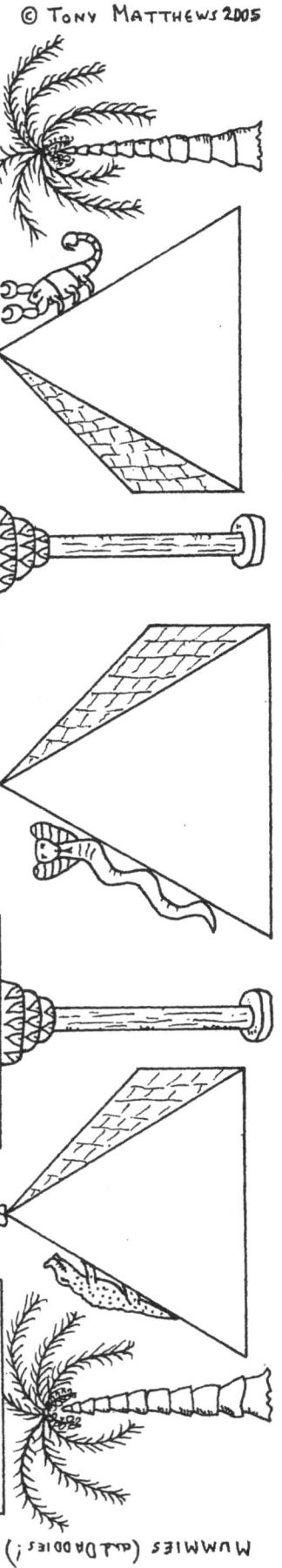

© Tony Matthews 2005

MUMMIES (and Daddies!)

BARROW HENGE

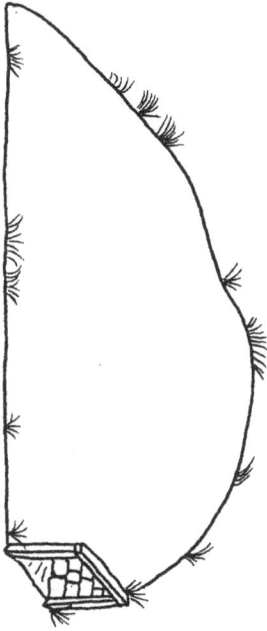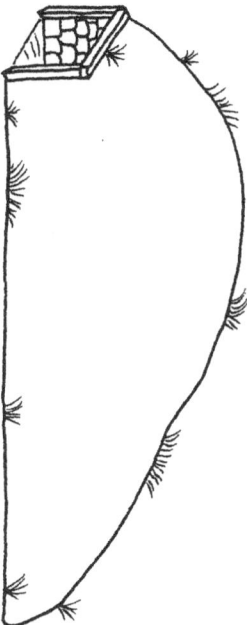

© Tony Matthews 2006

CAN YOU DIG IT ?

You find me in the standing stone,
And on a cyclopean wall.
I am one with pottery and bones,
That's if you find me at all.

In Druid chant and Wiccan spell,
I am heard on the wind.
And in Celtic jewelry as well,
Mounted, clasped, pinned.

You find me in weapon, tool, art,
In artifact and monument,
Hieroglyphics and runes in part,
In pyramids you catch my scent.

Archeo, paleo, and other ologists
Dig me up, puzzle my pieces.
Reconstruct me, make new lists,
In hypothesis, lecture, thesis.

I am Egyptian, Aztec and Incan,
Mayan, Australian, Phonecian,
Cambodian, Roman and Indian,
Grecian, Minoan, European.

I am in the trepanned skull,
And in the sacrificial heart.
I fought lions, danced the bull,
And rode dragons at the start.

The shaman sees me, in a trance,
Giants carry my coffin and grieve.
Fairies join me in a magic dance,
The gods see me, and believe.

Yet I still remain visible to all,
Who have but the grace to see,
And can heed the astral call.
Now you : do you know me ?

cont.

I walked with the apemen,
And wandered in Atlantis.
I planted the Tree in Eden,
And gave Nessie a big kiss.

I am in the temples and tumili,
Buried in mounds of earth,
In circles and seasons find me,
And know what I am worth.

In holy water and virgin's blood,
The gold illuminated manuscript,
Buried in bog or field of mud,
On peak and tor, valley or crypt.

In fossils of trilobite and dinosaur,
Stratas of rock, rings of trees.
I am on altar and mosaic floor,
Columns and painted frieze.

I am in the Ice Age's tide,
And the continental shifting.
I sailed the oceans wide,
And the mountains' uplifting.

In castle ditch and hearthplace,
In flint, bronze, iron, ivory,
In rivers and lakes see my face,
In dust and flames I may be.

King Arthur, Robin Hood and I
Told stories around the campfire,
And talked of days long gone by,
For myths and legends never tire.

I am in meaning and memory.
I am the soul understanding.
I am in you, and you are in me,
Our Ark will soon be landing.

cont.

The Equinox precedes me,
I emerge from the midden.
A volcano I might well be,
Of debitage, unbidden.

A phoenix from a pyre,
A comet of Eternity,
An earthquake of desire,
A Flood, and I am free.

I am a footprint in the rock,
On beach and cave am cast.
I am the ticking of a clock,
I am the Spirit of the Past.

****

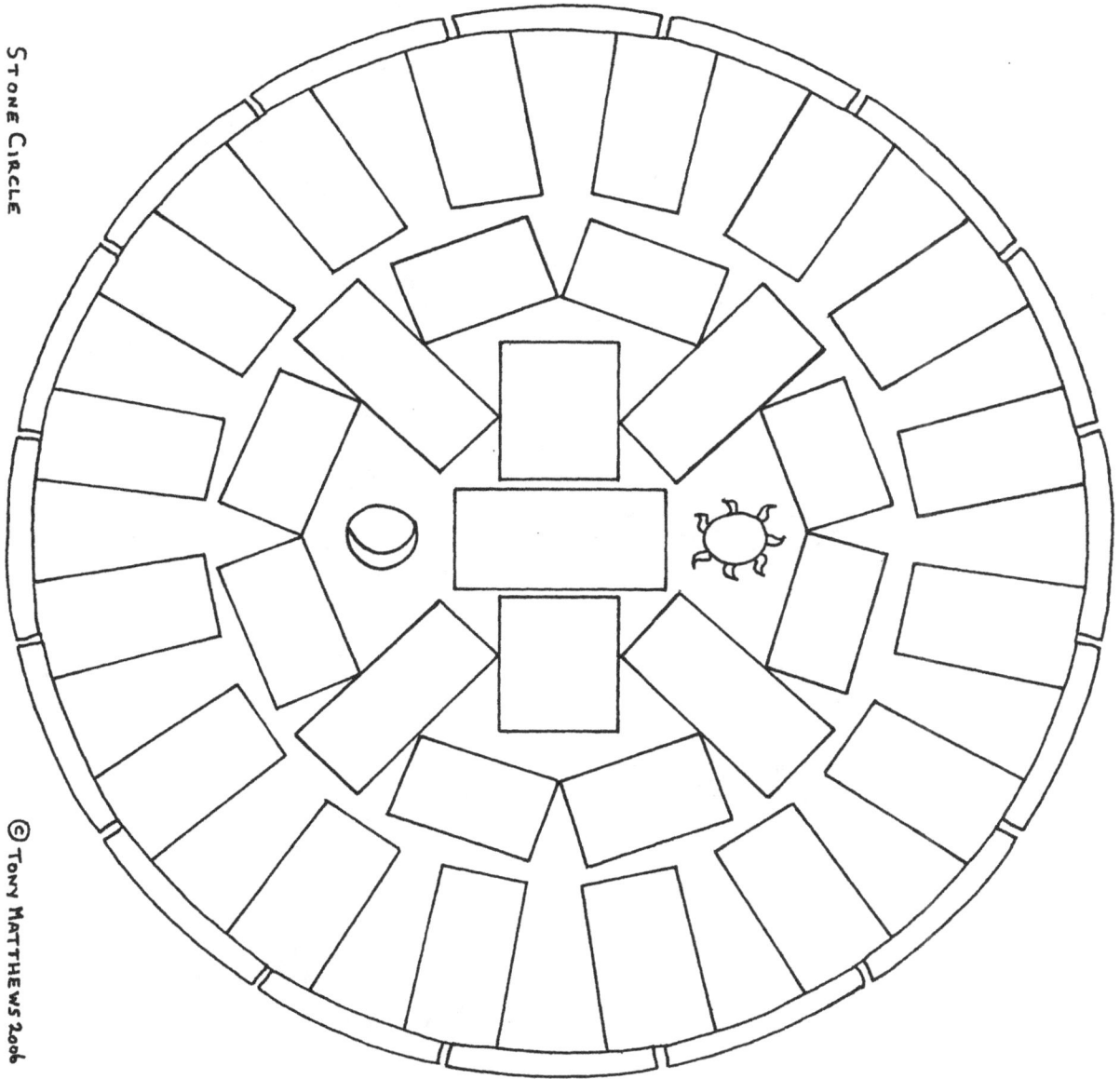

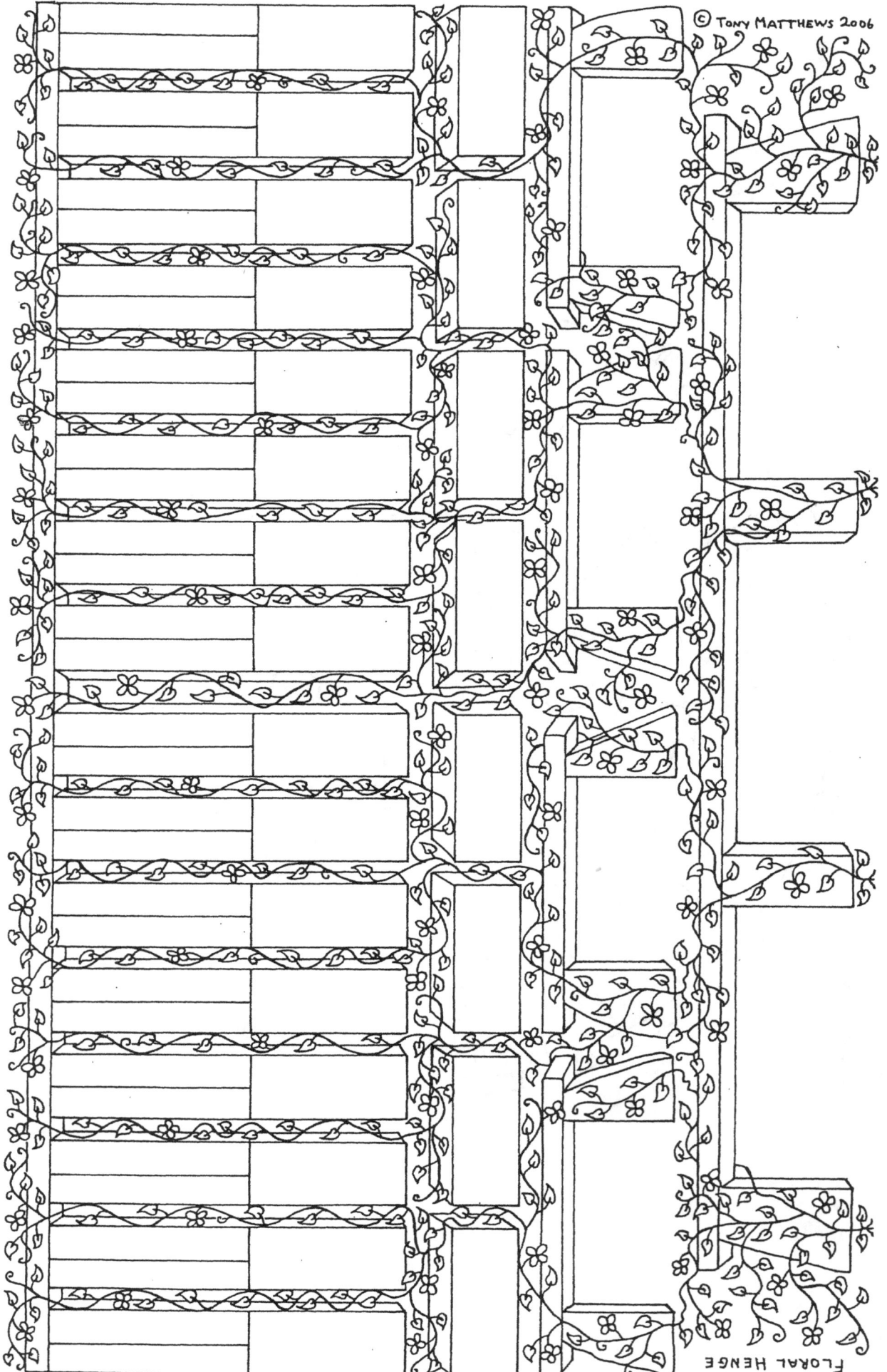

© Tony Matthews 2006

FLORAL HENGE

ARCHEOLOG

I was at Stonehenge for Solstice,
And at Angkhor Wat I prayed.
At Chichen Itza I saw the Eclipse,
And at Nazca I am arrayed.

They painted me at Lascaux,
I spiraled around New Grange.
I climbed up to find Cusco,
And Lake Titicata, very strange.

I got ahead on Easter Island,
Rode a white horse at Uffington.
Slid down glaciers in Iceland,
Swapped fishy tales with a Dogon.

I joined the queue at Carnac,
Was flint-hearted at Grime's Grave.
Went to Mesopotamia and back,
Got Sherwood arrows for to save.

The Sphinx was just a playful toy,
Like Beowulf's charming pet.
I've dug through the layers of Troy,
But not found El Dorado yet.

I was a perfect fit at Tiahuanaco,
At Skara Brae I was buried in sand.
Then played loud Jazz at Jericho,
And was heard over in Vinland.

I longed for a barrow at West Kennet,
Using an ankh for ever as my key.
Malta is not an easy place to forget,
And Silbury Hill's still a mystery.

All these places, and so many more,
I wonder just how they were built,
And what they were once built for,
And what else is under sea and silt.

cont.

Dracos or Orion rise over me,
With Sirius pointing the way.
A good calendar to guide me,
As Quetzacoatl comes today.

I babbled on in old Babylon,
Whispered omens at Delphi.
Found some healing in Avalon,
And stood around at Avebury.

I took the Glastonbury tour,
Was shooed at Weyland's Smithy.
Spoke Rosetta, you know what for,
And declared Tut as my mummy.

Got lost in the Bermuda Triangle,
Minotaur's Maze at Knossos too.
Was buried at Pompeii in a tangle,
Could never reach Machu Picchu.

Soloman greeted me solemnly,
But Prester John was hard-pressed.
So I searched through Zimbabwe,
And at a ziggurat took my rest.

I got the point when at Giza,
A rounded view of the Olmecs.
I explored the sewers of Sumer,
And Roman aquaducts were next.

Found the Milky Way at Teotihuacan,
Took the path up to the Parthenon.
Balanced on cromlechs and dolmen,
Saw the cliff Anasazi had moved on.

So my archeolog continues on,
And the Past comes back to me,
People and cultures long gone,
That still survive as our history.

****

© Tony Matthews 2006

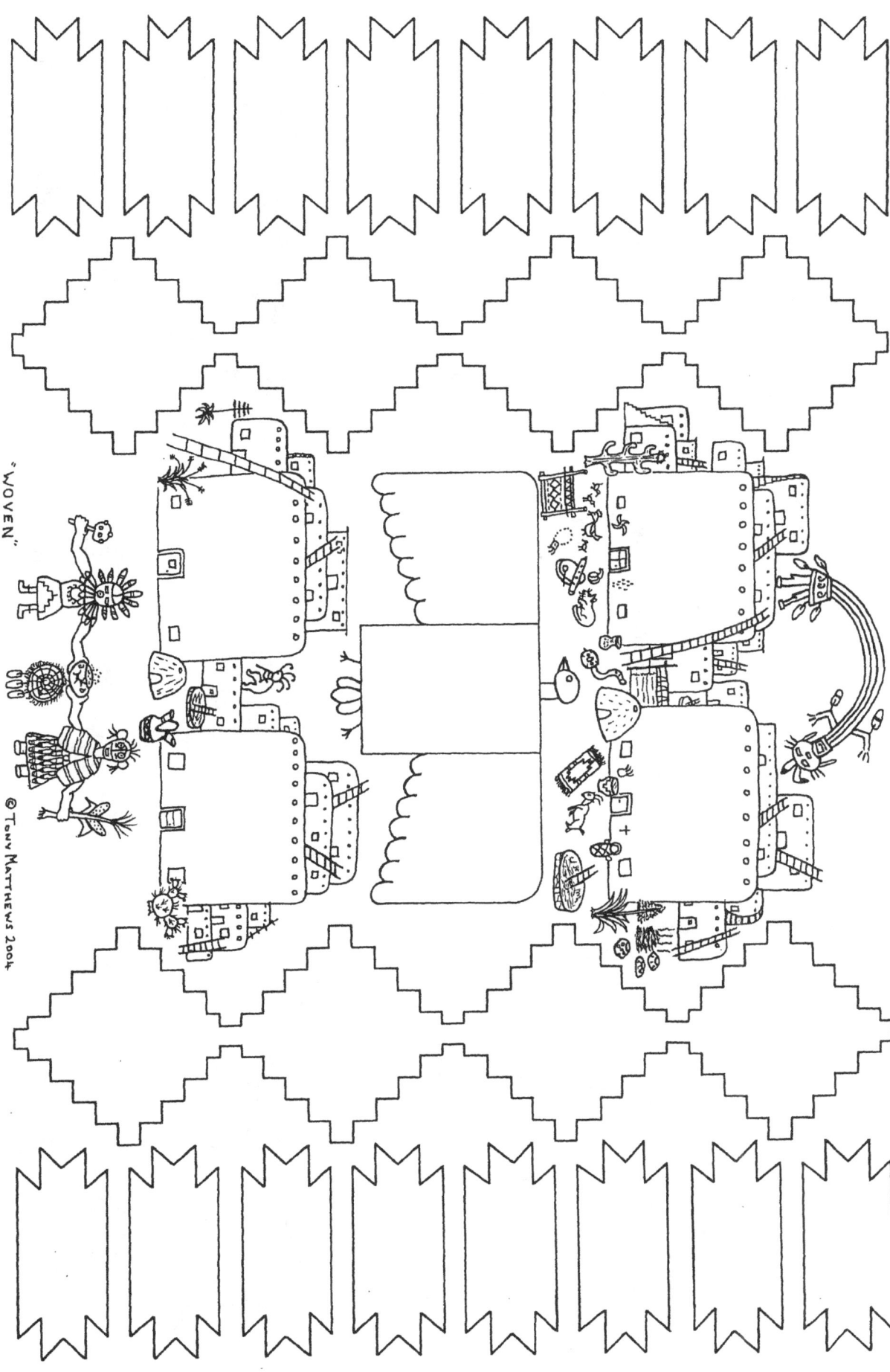

"WOVEN"

© Tony Matthews 2004

PARADISE

©Tony Matthews 2003

SSSSSTAMPEDE! ©2006 ©Tony Matthews

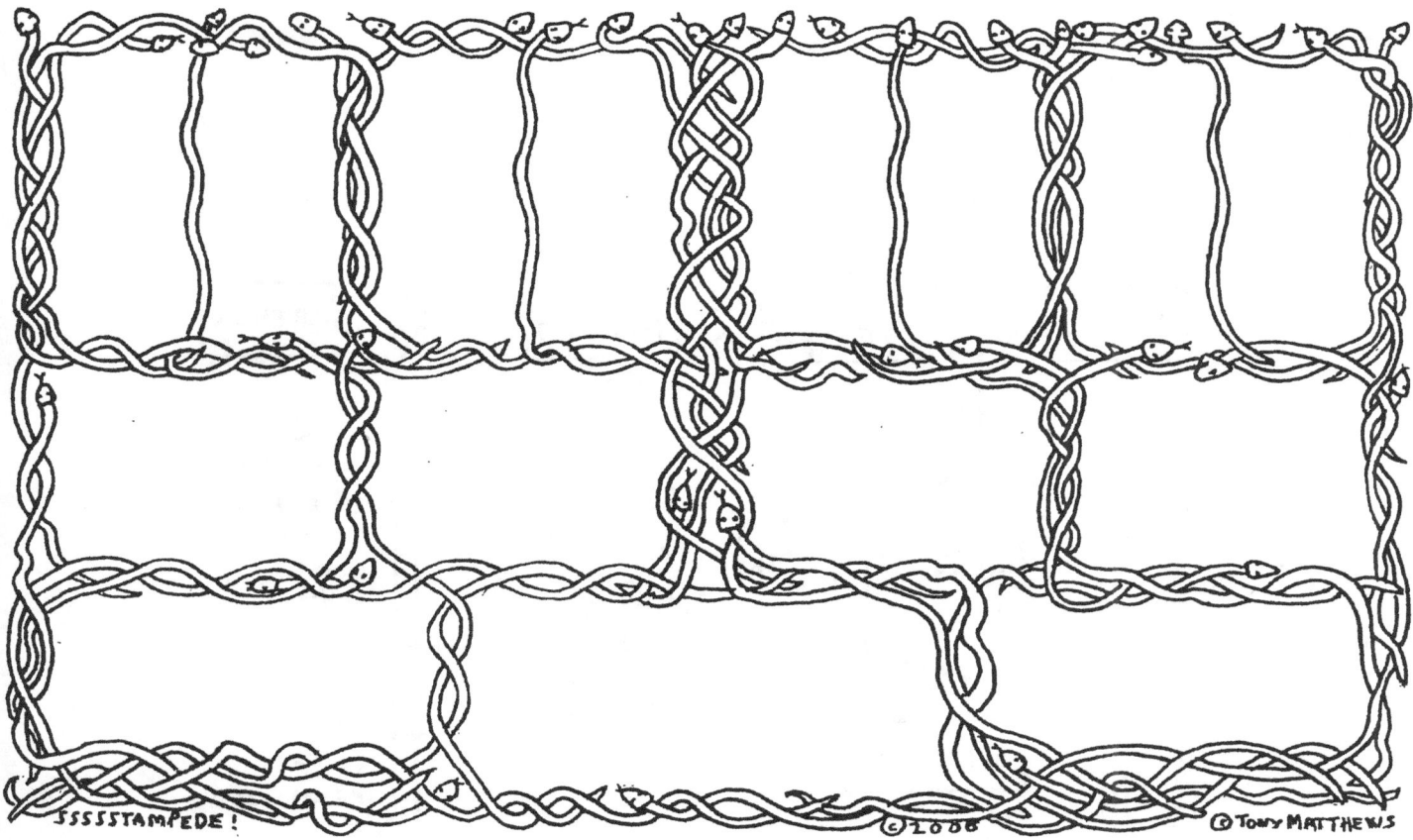

300 YEARS LATER.....

Great, that's it finally finished, now
remind me again what it's actually for.....

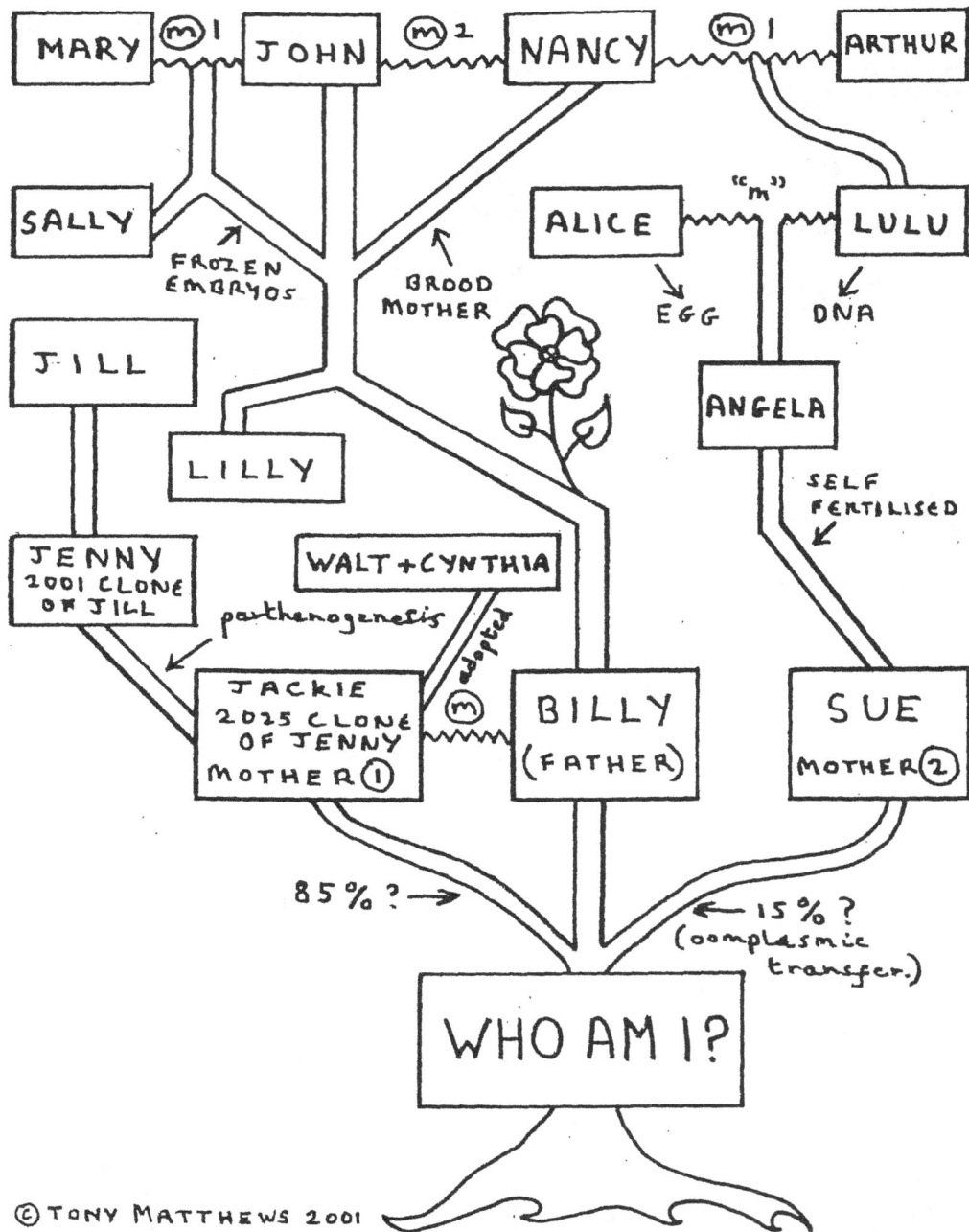

MARY ⓜ1 JOHN ⓜ2 NANCY ⓜ1 ARTHUR

SALLY

FROZEN
EMBRYOS

BROOD
MOTHER

ALICE ~"m"~ LULU

EGG DNA

JILL

ANGELA

SELF
FERTILISED

LILLY

JENNY
2001 CLONE
OF JILL

WALT + CYNTHIA

parthenogenesis

adopted

JACKIE
2025 CLONE
OF JENNY
MOTHER ①

ⓜ

BILLY
(FATHER)

SUE
MOTHER ②

85 % ? →

← 15 % ?
(ooplasmic
transfer.)

WHO AM I?

© TONY MATTHEWS 2001

Donate A Previous Spouse, Or Adopt A Clone.

Sounds a bit like a charity drive, but I don't want anyone to be left out. This is the special section where I will be dealing with Trees for special people, such as the adopted or those born of a sperm donor, who previously have had no Tree to use, or had to use the traditional one, and leave a lot of blank spaces. But there is a Tree for everyone, and I hope to fill some of the needs here.

I've kept to simple floral designs, but the emphasis is on the layout anyway. Anyone designing their own Tree can follow all of the previous ideas in this, and my other books, when it comes to what images you use.

Pay Attention, Please.

This is where you need to keep your wits about you, for not all of the following designs are Trees/bloodlines/pedigrees, etc. Some are, some aren't. I've tried to mark each one clearly to show what the design is for. This is vital, so that future generations are aware of what they are looking at. For example, with a baby born from a sperm donor, he will have 2 dads on his design.....the one who raised him, and the one who's DNA he carries. There's a big difference.

Odd One Out.

Let me deal with this odd one out first. It's called Morf 21, the full title being MaleORFemale 21 generations. In fact it is not odd at all, for it is simply a way of showing a direct bloodline going back for 21 generations. You can use it in 3 different ways. First is your male/surname/Y-chromosome line going back from you to your dad, to his dad, to his dad......

Then you could use it for your female/X-chromosome line from you to your mum, to her mum, to her mum......

Finally (and this explains the title), you can swap to and fro between the male and female lines. They have to be direct ancestors, no straying off to uncles or great aunts. But it could go something like this : you (on the bottom right), then across left your dad (who the line comes through) and his spouse (your mum). Then you go up and right to, say, your dad's mum (who the line comes through) and her spouse. Then up left to her mum and spouse, then up right to her dad and spouse, then up left to his dad and spouse.....once you get the idea, it is obvious. What you are doing is simply following a trail through a regular 21 generation pedigree chart, but leaving out all of the great greats etc. who are not on the direct line to, say, your famous Admiral ancestor. It's a bit like following a river back from the sea (you), branching off into a tributary, then into one of the several streams that feed that tributary, and on until you come to the spring that starts that particular stream. You could then throw a packet of food dye (let's use a symbolic blood red dye) into that spring, and watch the colour flow back to the sea where you started.

Of course, the colour will be a bit thin by then, but then so is the blood of that famous, or infamous, ancestor after 21 generations.

5 Donations.

Yet only 2 trees. 4 are identical except for the way that they are marked, and the fact that some are pedigree, and some are not.

The first is straightforward. Say a woman has some defect/illness/operation that has affected her womb. Still, her eggs are good. Some are removed, and hubby's (or should I say "partner's", to be politically correct?) sperm added. The resulting embryo is then implanted in a second woman's womb....the surrogate mother, and brought to term. This surrogate mother surely deserves a place on the tree, even if none of her DNA is involved. After all, she did all of the hard work!

For the second tree it's the man who is having problems. He is infertile. Thus we go to a sperm donor, and the wife for the resulting embryo (in the laboratory, or behind closed doors). Hubby deserves to be on the tree for he will be "dad" to the child, and he's probably paying for the whole thing, financially and/or emotionally. His wife gets to do the hard work again, and she and her DNA are on the tree, of course, but so is the sperm donor. Regardless of whether he meets the couple, or not, it's his DNA that is there too. This might be important if you were studying inherited traits or illnesses.

The above are both in the 1-3-6-12 formats, as is the third version, though this could also appear in the later section on the adopted.....here we have a single mother who gives up (donates) her baby for adoption. (Or maybe, for various reasons that you may imagine for yourself, the father is unknown.). Here I simply show the actual mother, and the two adopter parents.

The fourth in this set is a more recent development. You will notice that the child has two mothers. No, neither of us are drunk, there really are two mothers. And there are already several hundred kids of this persuasion around already. It comes from an infertility treatment where, in non-technical terms, the batteries in a woman's egg are flat. Imagine a chicken's egg, and the batteries (mitochondria) float around in the white. So batteries are drawn from another woman's egg, added to the first woman's, and the engines are up and running. The minor detail is that some DNA comes along with the batteries, and appear in the child, along with mum and dad's.....thus we have the Extra DNA Donor that deserves a place on the tree.

The fifth tree moves us into the near Future (or maybe the near Past, I don't always keep up). It is possible to "fertilize" an egg using genetic material rather than sperm. In this version " Gaily Onward" I am thinking of a lesbian couple who, using this technique, might be able to have each other's child.

Let's add 3 more trees to this list. By the same technique a woman might even have her own self-fertilized baby

Then we have clones hovering on the horizon. Is he your son/daughter or brother/sister? What are the legal ramifications of inheritance from your parents, or between him and your natural son?

Finally, a lighter touch, a tree for a test tube baby.

SURROGATE MOTHER

SPERM DONOR

EGG DONOR

DONOR TREE

©Tony Matthews 2005

Donor Tree

SPERM DONOR

NATURAL MOTHER

HUSBAND

©Tony Matthews 2005

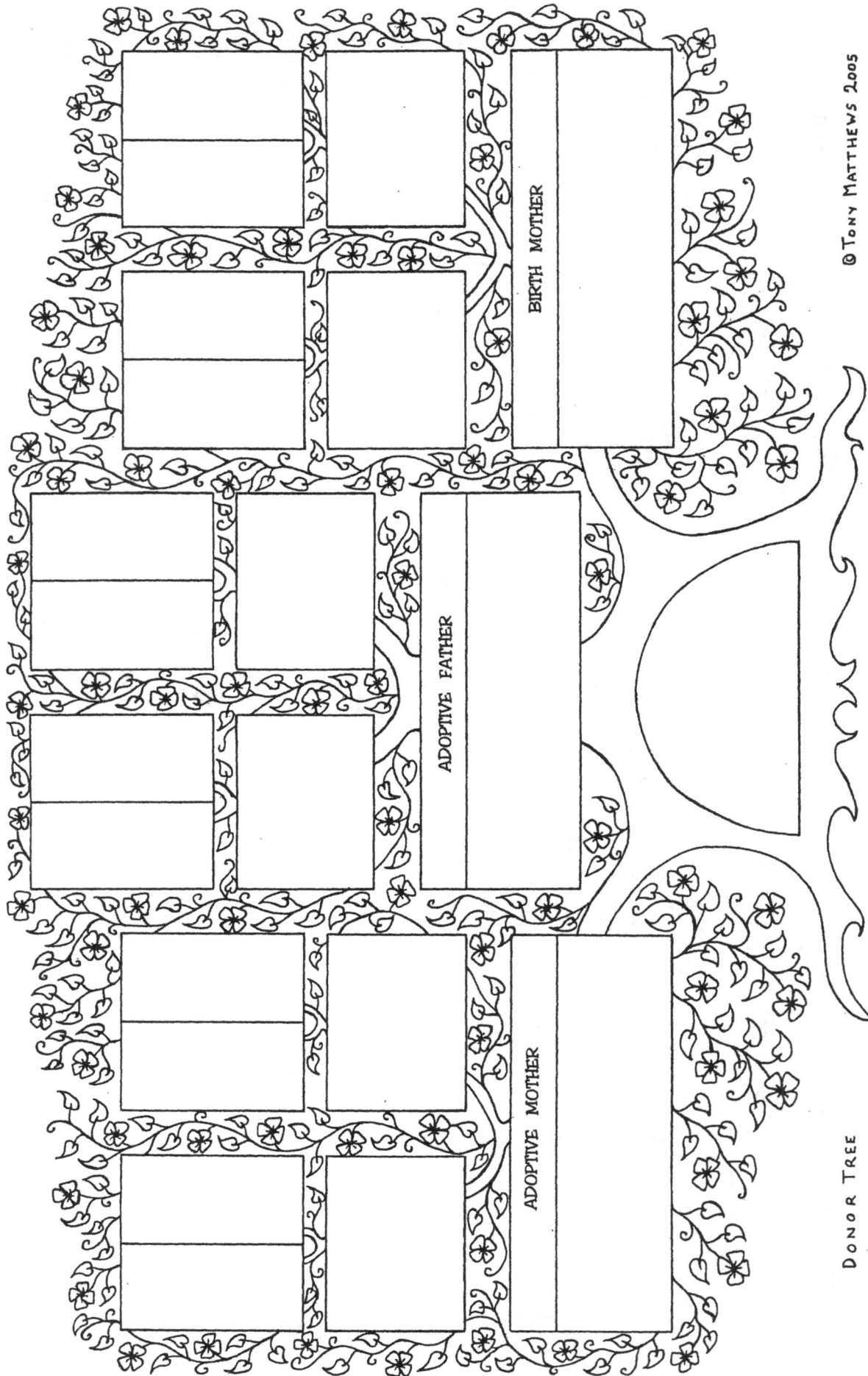

BIRTH MOTHER

ADOPTIVE FATHER

ADOPTIVE MOTHER

Donor Tree

©Tony Matthews 2005

DONOR TREE

BIRTH MOTHER

NATURAL FATHER

EXTRA DNA DONOR

© Tony Matthews 2005

© Tony Matthews 2005

BIRTH MOTHER

GENETIC DONOR

GAILY ONWARD

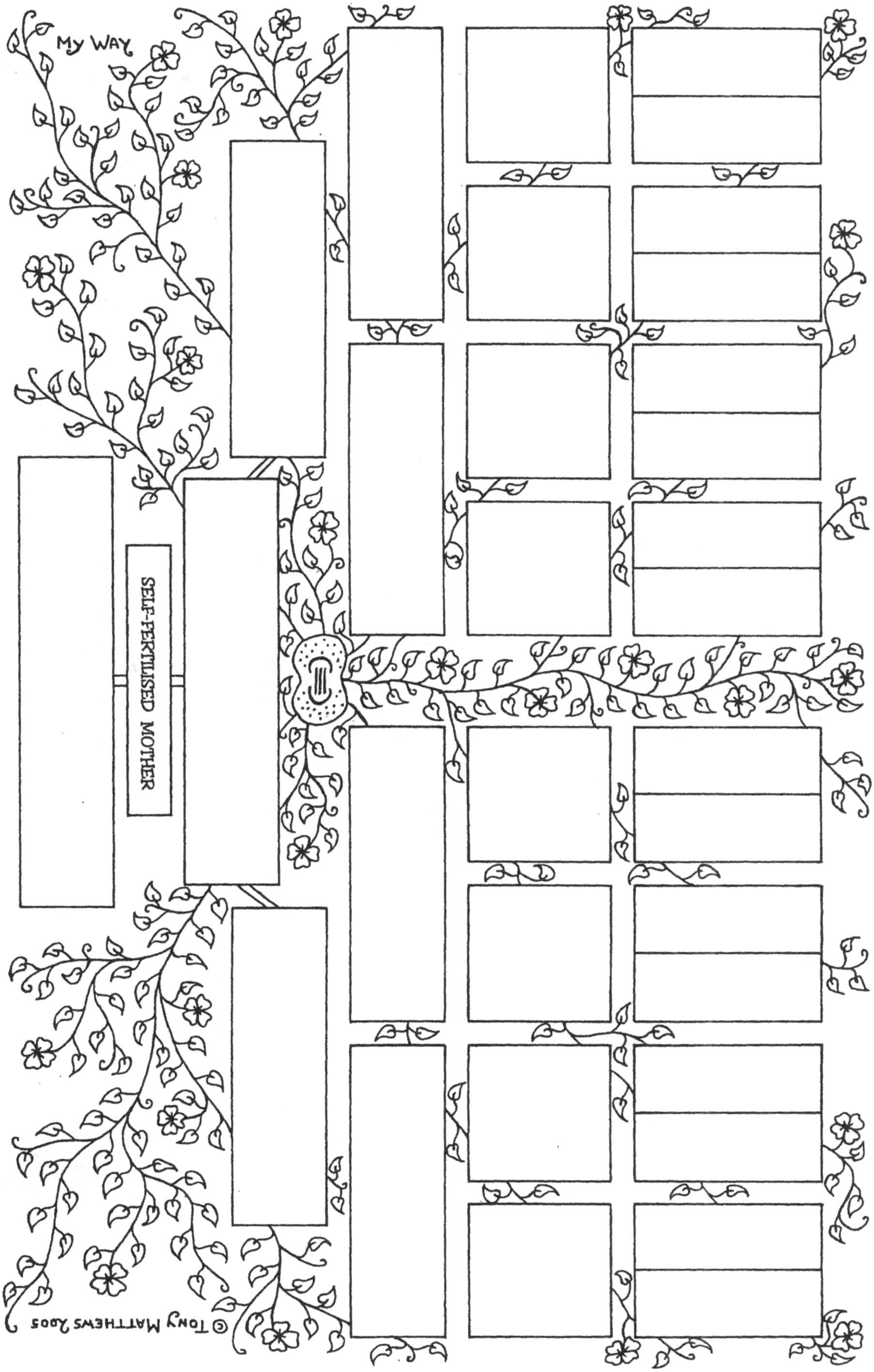

My Way
SELF-FERTILISED MOTHER
© Tony Matthews 2005

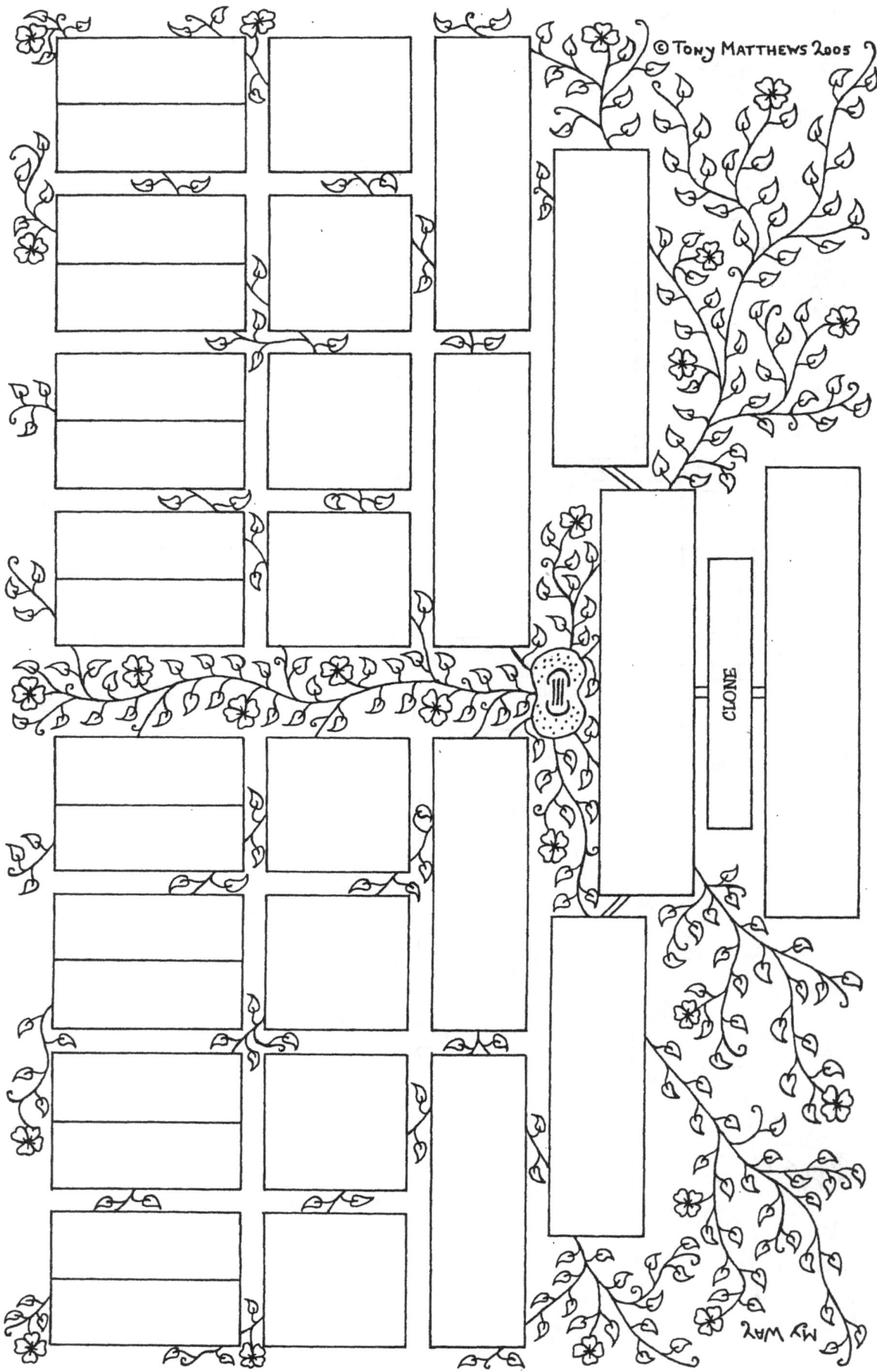

© Tony Matthews 2005

CLONE

My Way

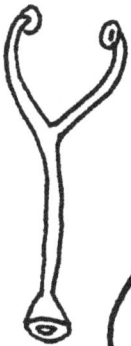

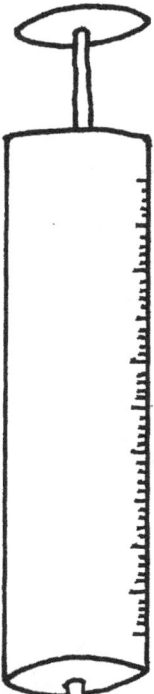

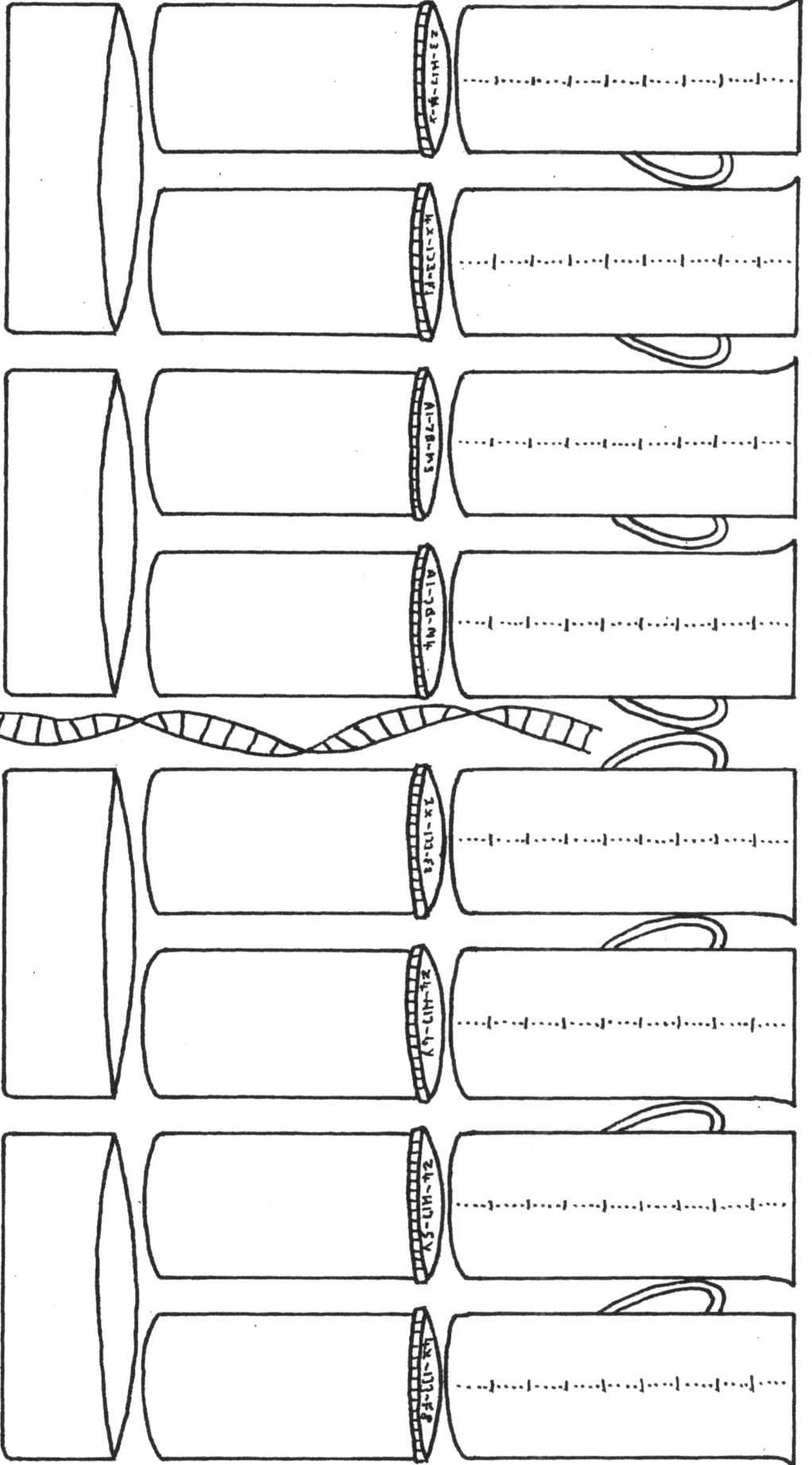

Sharing.

The next little section comprises 2 trees for previous marriages, and 3 for adopted people.

First is "Shared Experience". This is for a man or a woman who is married with children, but who has had a previous spouse, also with resulting children. I use the terms spouse and marriage, but you might want to use partner and partnership. The result is the same, for you have two sets of kids who are half-siblings to each other.

The second tree takes this concept further. In "Gently Used" we have a couple with children, but who both have children from a previous marriage. Here's an odd situation, in a pedigree sense, for his previous and current children are half-siblings. Her previous and current kids are half-siblings. But what relationship is there between his and her previous children ?

Let's move on to adopted people. It's very understandable that they want their adopters to be recognized and remembered, although there is no DNA involved. If they find out who their natural parents are, then they may want to celebrate this too, and not only for reasons such as inherited traits or illnesses, but for finding other family members, etc. Thus the first tree, "Adoptree", simply shows the child with all four "parents", and their ancestors.

Then we move on to the people I've mentioned earlier who haven't done a tree because half of it would be blank. Here are two balanced trees that have an adopted person on it. The first case is someone who is adopted, but who has a spouse and children. Thus this is "Their Tree", for it shows the children, the adopted person, the spouse and his/her parents, grandparents, etc.

The third case is for those who say that their mum or dad was adopted. Again, they themselves have a spouse and children. Thus "Adoparent" shows the children, then the couple, then that couple's parents, one of whom was adopted. From there we trace the other 3 parents back to their parents and grandparents.

With these last 2 trees you will notice that I've carefully put in lines to indicate who is parent of who. We could go further, and incorporate the adopter parents into such as the last 2 trees, but I think that it would start to get confusing, though it is indeed possible with a little thought given to the layout, to keep it balanced, and to very careful marking to show which are pedigree lines, and which aren't. Eventually we may want combinations of all of these special trees !

The Rest.

There are other Trees in this book, but hopefully they need little explanation. These are where I've tried to use a theme for a whole Tree, and thus you have the Pyramids, or vegetables or Stonehenge, as well as stained glass, actual trees, flowers and aliens. Then there's a section of Trees based around one object such as a pear, nautilus, fish, or a train. And a couple of others that are "one-offs". My constant theme, though, is to demonstrate and suggest how all sorts of images may be used to create a Tree that describes you and your family. I can only encourage you to have a go…..and I'd love to see your result !

SHARED EXPERIENCES

FIRST SPOUSE

SECOND SPOUSE

FIRST SPOUSE

FIRST SPOUSE

ADOPTREE

ADOPTIVE PARENTS

NATURAL PARENTS

© Tony Matthews. 2005

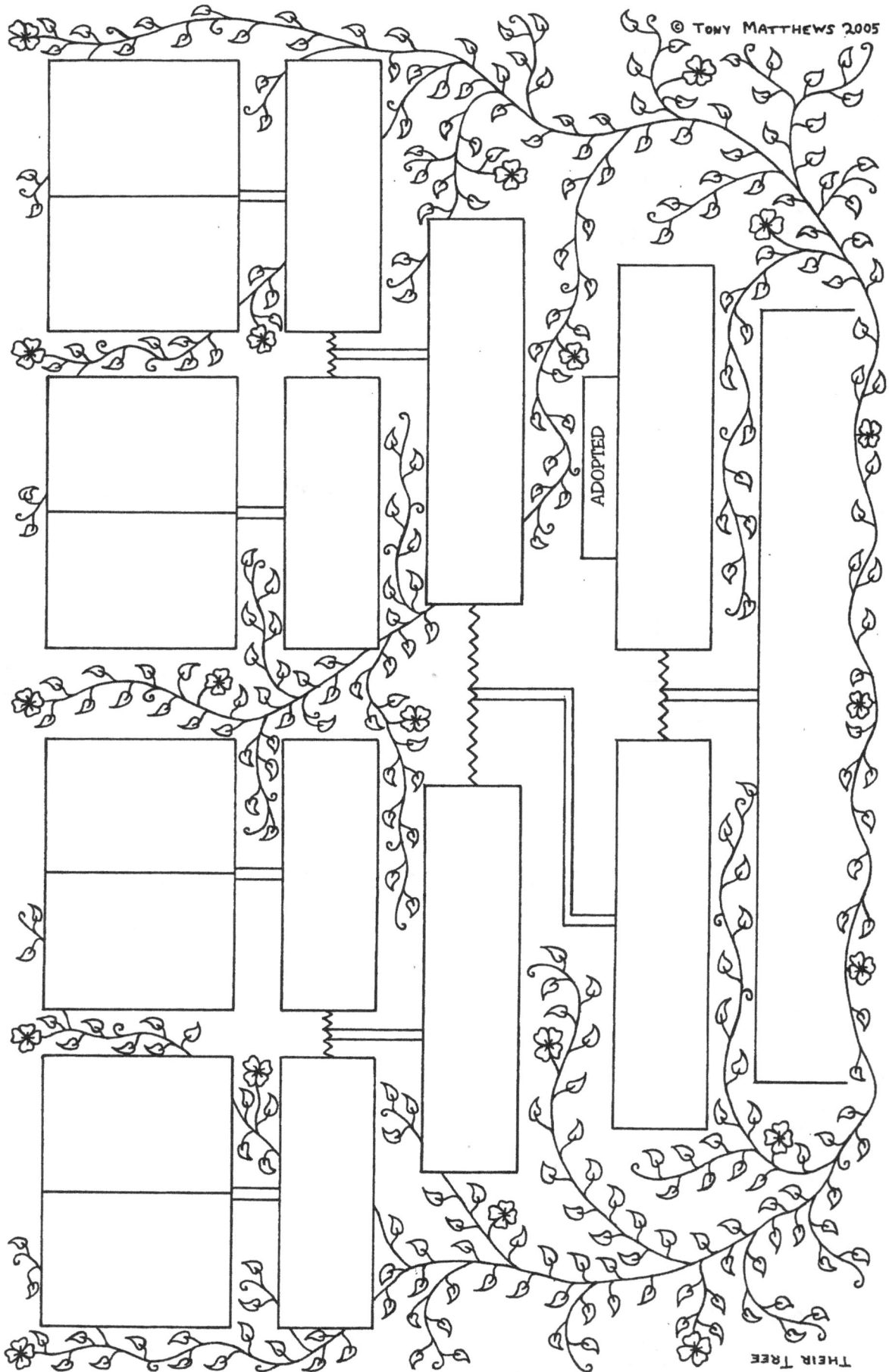

© Tony Matthews 2005

ADOPTED

THEIR TREE

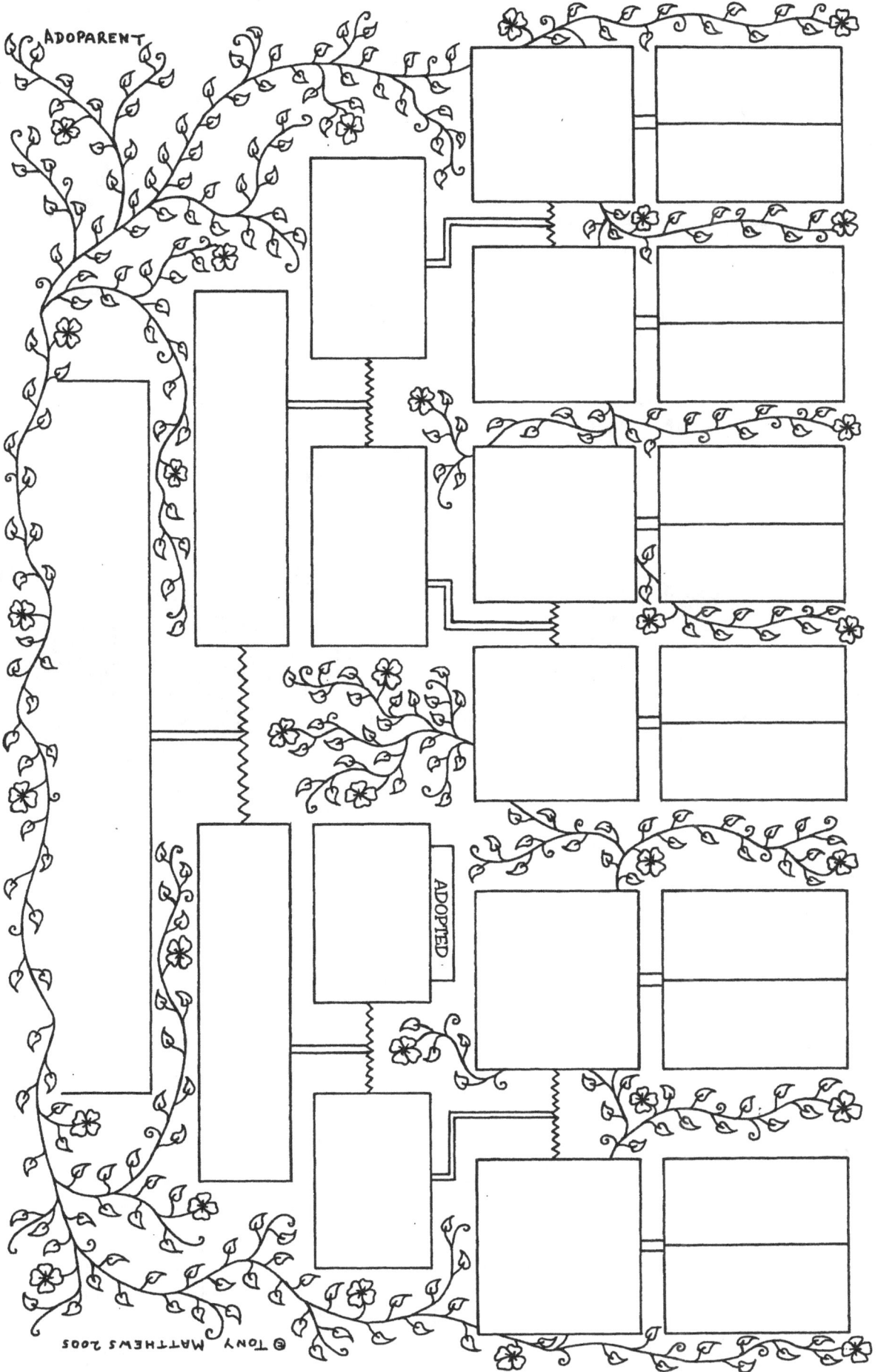

ADOPARENT

ADOPTED

© TONY MATTHEWS 2005

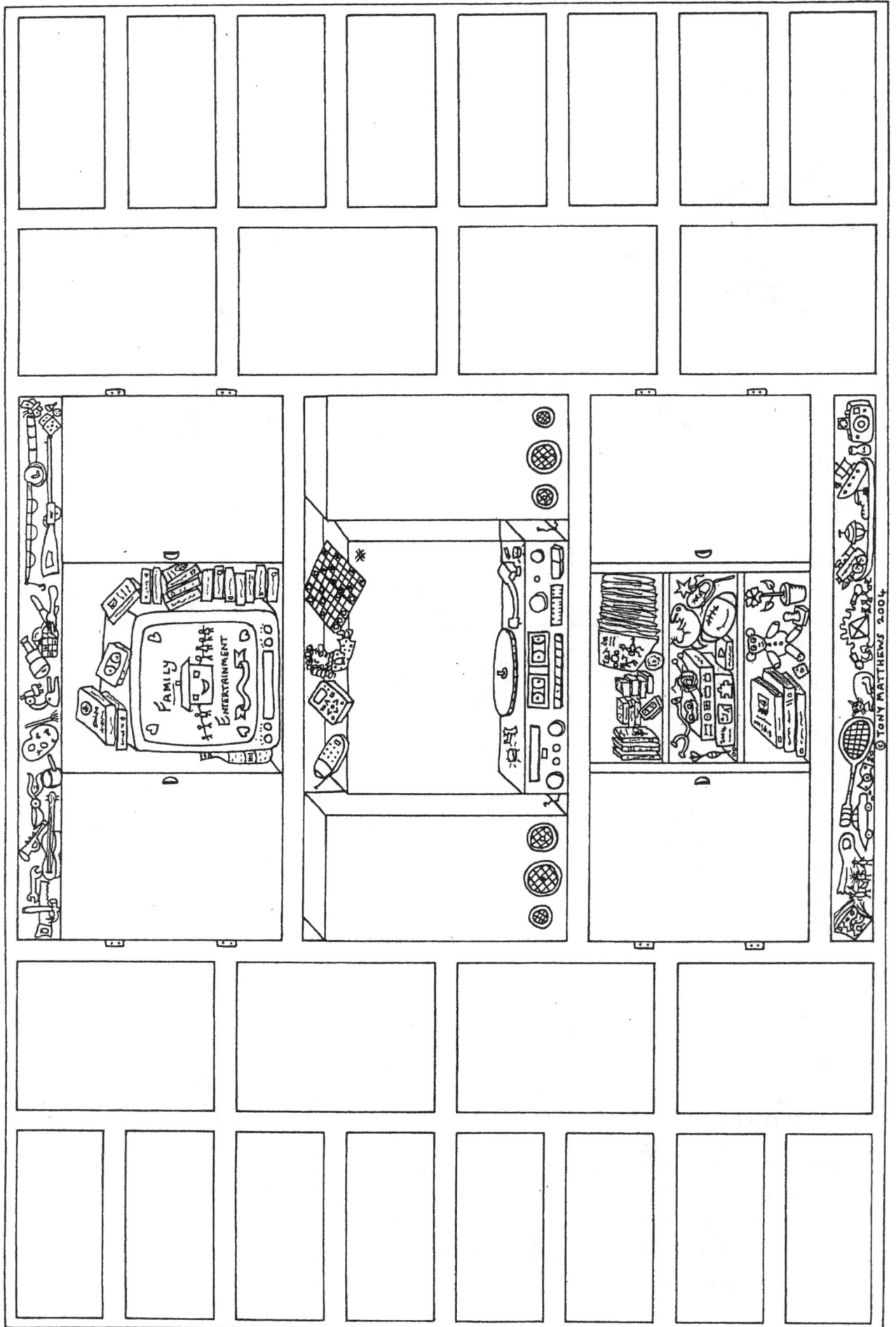

© TONY MATTHEWS 2004

FAMILY PLAZA

C'mon guys, pleeeeeease tell me where
you've hidden my Time Machine.

Come quick, and watch, Honey.
It's time for the next Ice Age.

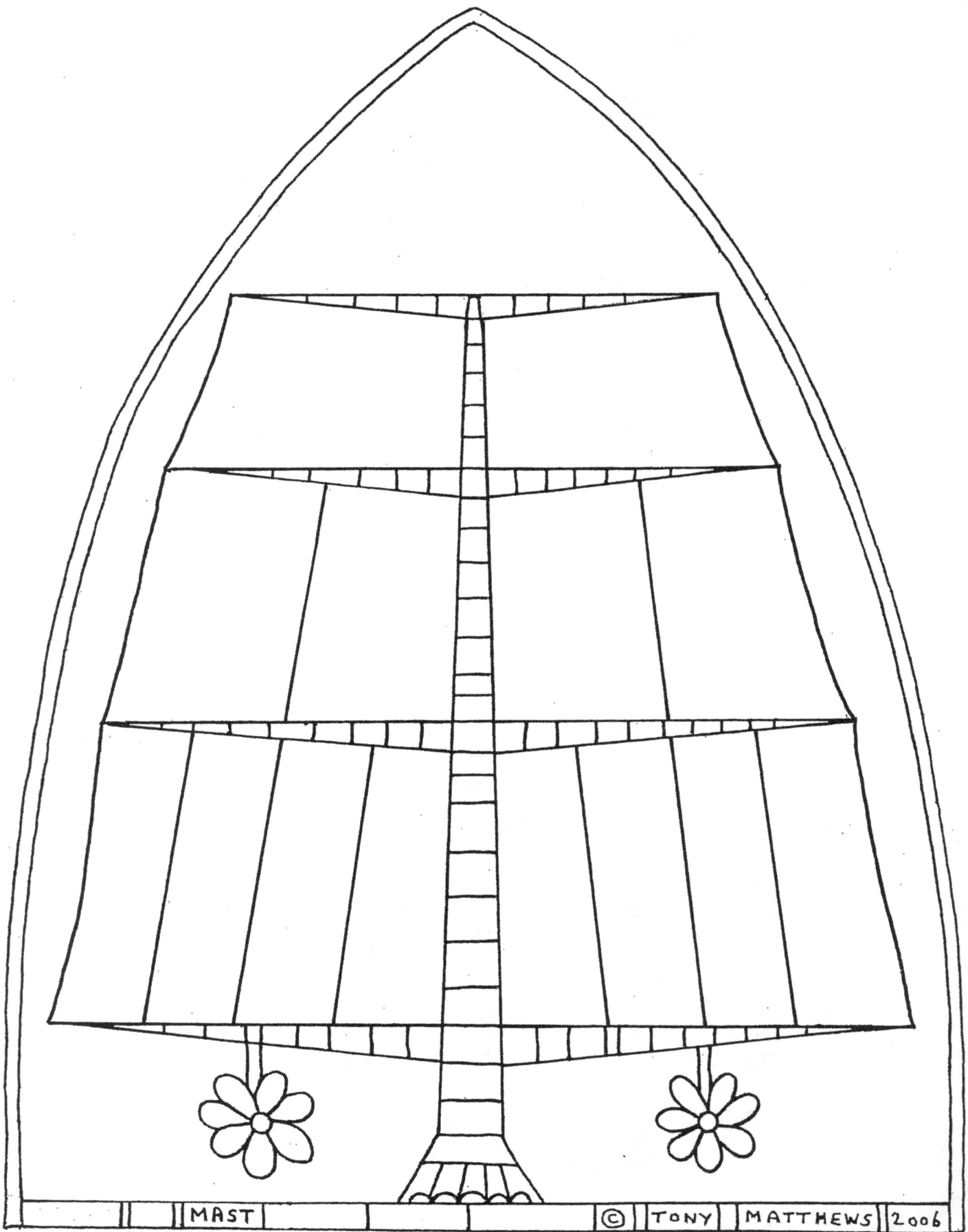

MAST   © TONY MATTHEWS 2006

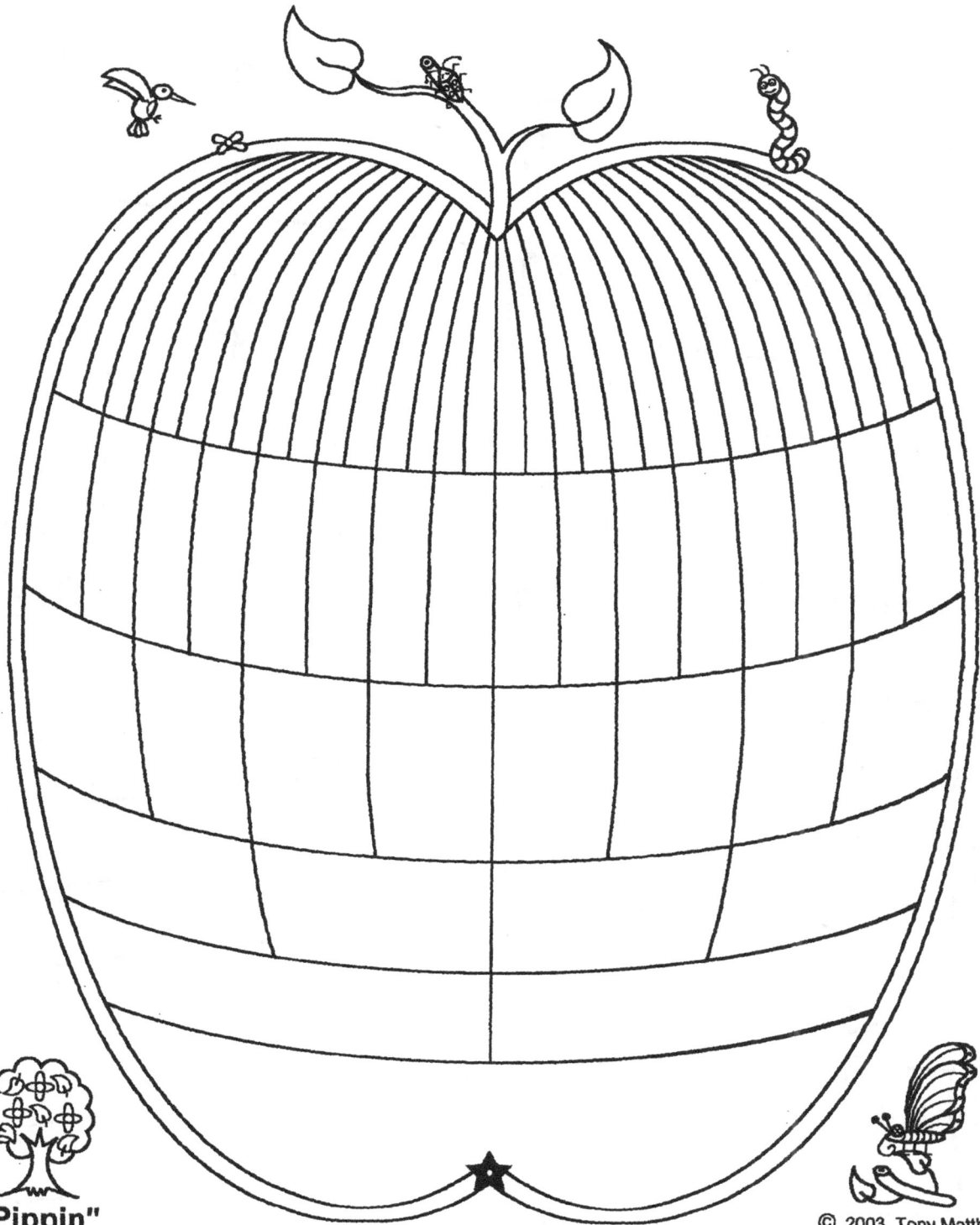

"Pippin"

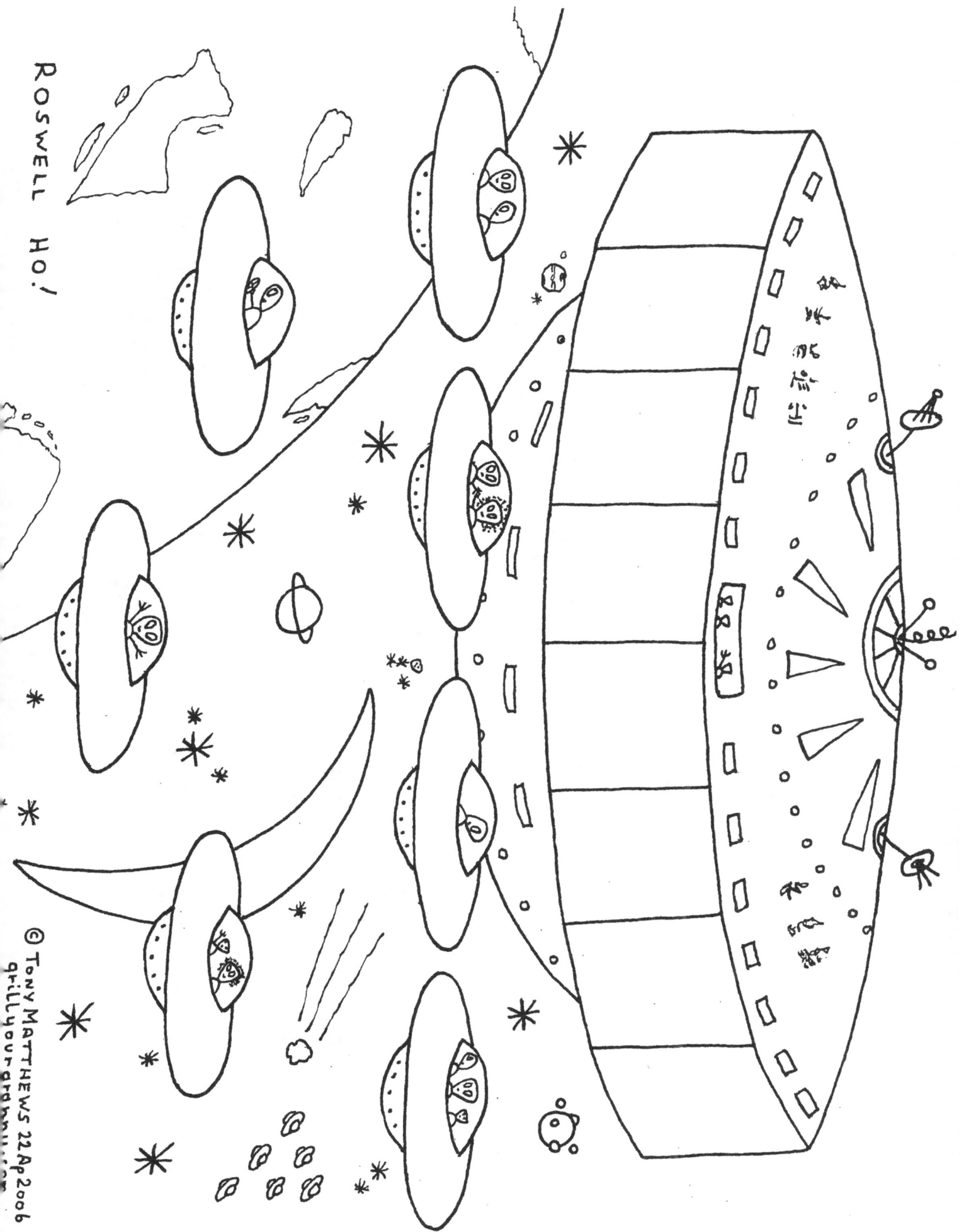

ROSWELL HO!

© Tony Matthews 22 Ap 2006
grillyourgrandma.com

Recipe For Success.

I've subtitled this book " A Feast Of Family Trees", and, indeed, I hope that you will feast your eyes on the designs. But think also of the analogy of a cookbook, with recipes and ingredients. You are the chef. My layouts and images are only a clue to what treets you can come up with for your family. Everyone's taste is different. Some ingredients are suitable for various layouts (the equivalent of bake, boil, or fry), and you cooks and gourmets will recognize that, say, a fish can be baked, boiled or fried. Likewise the image of a fish.

I have shown one with the boxes inside it. You could use a school of fish just as I used vegetables, writing each name within the shape of each fish. Then again, think of an island, and have your fish swimming around the outside as in Your Frame, or even jump in amongst them by using Your Path. A single fish could work on Your Shape, or a photo with you and that 100lb catfish could adorn the centre of Your Pic. Who knew just how versatile fish could be ! I'm feeling hungry already.

Smell something fishy ? Dozens of other images could be used instead, in exactly the same way. You might go for dinosaurs or cars, apples or hearts, or any shape that you can write a name in. Some shapes you can't, of course, but then you don't normally fry jello.

Let's say that you are into guns, or tools. Okay, well you can still easily do a border of revolvers or pliers. There are clip-art books and cds with historical weapons and implements. You might use a horizontal rifle and write your name above it, or a photo of your favourite sledgehammer could be used as Your Pic. You could combine the Your Path idea, but add a border, and do a whole collection of stuff.

Obviously Trees like the Egyptian, Stonehenge, or Pueblo style that I've done take a little more imagination, but then some of you might be artists, and I'd like to inspire you too.

I've given suggestions as to where you might get your ingredients, such as clip-art, and really, the simplest way is to just go and browse just as you would at a food market. See what catches your eye, or your kid's, You know what they are like when you take them shopping, if you ask them what they would like for supper. They may choose pizza and cookies. Okay, so treet them....in my analogy you could help them to do a Tree such as Your Frame with images of pizza and cookies as the border. Or in the vegetable style use cookies as the shapes to write your name in. Then you could get really exotic and look at Stone Circle....can you see a pizza there ? Anyway, he's going to lick his lips every time that he sees that Tree. What better way of learning ?

Of course, you might be a prudent housewife, and want to prepare a shopping list first, before going out. I don't know what your particular hobby, career, or characteristic is, but I do know that just about everything comes with associated images, or photos, (and in some cases text, which can also be used) that can become a Tree using my layouts.

What's For Dinner Tonight ?

Let's say that you, like many people, have some ag labs or farmers in your ancestral background. Try to picture a farm, and see what images spring to mind, for they will all be good ingredients for a Farm Pie Tree, as it were.

I can immediately think of the animals that they might have raised such as pigs, cows, horses, sheep, chickens, or goats. They used machinery and tools such as a tractor, carts, scythes, hay rake and fork, plough, spade, post-hole digger, and much more. There were various barns, stables, drying sheds, coops, fences, feed bins and silos. You can probably add to this list. How about a sheaf of wheat or a haystack, and other crops and vegetables ?

Most of the above are easy to find as clip-art, etc., and are perfectly suitable for using in your recipe. The spade might be best as part of the border, but a cow or a barn could be written on, or have the squares inside, or work on my other varieties of layouts.

Lots of folk work in an office. You might be able to do a clever version of a shipping form that incorporates a Tree, but anyway there are images to pluck from and around your desk that range from phone, computer and typewriter, to pens, paper clips and stapler, the desk itself, and a chair, filing cabinets, in-tray, notepad, coffee mug.....some of these shapes are more versatile, but even a border would be fun, with your sheet of paper as your desk, with the name boxes in the centre, and all of your usual bits and pieces framing them.

Hobbies and collections are a great theme to use. Careers say a lot about you. Even a big interest such as football, classical music, history, science fiction, or gardening is great. All these come with associated images that you could use.

You might want to keep to one simple theme, but if your family were all into different things then you may want to go as far as using a separate image for each person, or simply use a border with a whole medley of things.

It might be fun to talk to aunts, cousins, parents, etc., to gather your ideas, and to scout for images. Their input and encouragement will spur you on, and the finished Tree should bring up some interesting conversations and memories. I've mentioned kids several times, but on a stick, cut or paste level. Many youngsters nowadays are more conversant with computers than you are. Send them "out" hunting online for images, or get their help in filling in names onscreen. They'll probably enjoy showing off their talents, and soak up some family history at the same time. They have become a little bored with you telling them how you only had a hoop, ball, "stick" gun, or skipping rope as a kid, but go back a generation or two and tell stories of those now gone, their struggles and triumphs, or something unusual that they did, or that happened to them. If you've a rogue amongst your ancestors that will have them pricking up their ears. I've found that a few stories tossed in casually can pique their interest, and they will soon be asking you questions. A simple way to start would be to mention that you are drawing up a Tree, and wonder what image they might like you to use for them. Who could resist such a question ?

So I says to him oh that, that's just a boil, and he says to me no, it's the mark of the devil, and I says nonsense, it's just a boil. All I need is some lavender oil, grave dust, wing of bat, and virgin's blood, and it'll be gone, but he says to me you're in league with the devil, you've sold your soul, and I says nonsense, I only sell love potions and the odd curse or poison, and then.....is it me, or is it getting hot in here ?......anyway, he says to me.........

Yoooo - hoooooo ! Hadrian !

Well, it had better not rain
until I've got my washing dry !

I'm going to miss the glaciers when they're gone.

Final Thoughts.

Well, I hope that I've inspired you to have a go at doing your Tree. There are quick and easy versions as I know how busy life can get. Then again, some of you will enjoy spending more time on it as you would on a quilt, jigsaw puzzle, model airplane, or crossword. Like any creative effort there are rewards both in your personal satisfaction and sense of achievement, as well as the kudos and involvement and praise of the rest of the family. Then there's also the serious underlining reason of helping to preserve your unique family history.

However, I've found that doing Trees can simply be fun, and there's always room for a little of that.

But There's More.

You may have noticed that I've only been talking about paper Trees, with a brief mention of computers....but some of you have other talents that you might bring to the table for the feast.

Might that Tree be set under the glass top of that table ?

I haven't seen (felt) a Braille Tree yet. Stained glass is an old tradition. Then there is metal scrollwork combined with (name) tiles.

But how about cloth and thread, could you quilters and needlers use these layouts ? In fact I know you can. I have an embroidered piece based on one of my floral fan designs. Then for quilting, well, you are using boxes and simple shapes already, and most of the designs in this book are based on boxes. Your names could thus go on a shape, not necessarily sewn, but at least on plainish coloured material using different coloured permanent markers. Then the spaces filled with (patterned ?) material such as you would regularly use. For greater effect you could start cutting up grandma's wedding dress, your first pinafore dress, one of dad's old gunny sacks and the sails from his yacht, or any other cloth relic. What a family keepsake that could be ! Perhaps your old bones aren't up to sewing anymore, but you could do a replica of a quilt idea by simply gluing the material onto a large board. Collages are interesting to play with too.

What might be done with wood ? Well, you could do a Tree on a door, I suppose. But how about something fancier ? I see a wooden upright, with crossbars. From these hang name shingles. You could drape the whole thing in plastic flowers or objects particular to your family....and, hey, you could even use it for your Christmas Tree !

How about paint and canvas ? The Michaelangelos amongst you could use any of my ideas, but on canvas instead of paper. Or you might like to try writing in the names, then just do abstract splashes of colour, and maybe glue on a few photos. Don't limit yourself, or be afraid to try. You might just surprise yourself (and everyone else). I know many people who would deny being creative, perhaps thinking of writing a novel or painting a Mona Lisa, but who have come up with perfectly charming pictures, models, garden beds, pottery, meals, cakes, dress designs, or something else.....creativity can take many forms, and some of these can be applied to making Trees. You and your skills immortalized.

" Look, son, here's a Family Tree that your grandpa did out of empty milk containers, the cardboard centres from toilets rolls, flattened soda cans, a bunch of nails, broken floral plates, string, and some old whitewash and left-over food dyes. Neat, huh ? What an inventive mind he had. ". " Wow, yeah. Wish I'd met him, he sounds like a great dad to have had. What else did he do ? ".

You don't have to stick to regular materials. Another interesting idea, that you might have seen a scrapbooker do, is to do your Tree on (fancy?) paper, with a blank border, and use a deep wooden frame. Then you can glue on some momentoes that might otherwise languish at the back of a drawer. You might have a lock of hair, a favourite toy car, pressed flowers, an old passport photo, a silver spoon, a medal, a concert ticket, or any of a thousand other little bits of paraphernalia to add to the uniqueness of your design.

Scrapbookers have a lot of other toys too, from printed borders, corners, and images, to wavy scissors, cut-out shapers, print wheels, paper embossers, shaped punches and more. There are printed strips (and clip-art) of floral or geometric designs, celtic knotwork and so on that could be used easily and effectively as dividers between the boxes. There are fancy capital letters to start the name in each box....why should they have all of the fun ? Your Tree could be a mini memory album. They, of course, might want to steal your ideas, and add Trees to their albums, and you could help, and share with, each other. These decorative ideas could also be used when designing title pages for individual family files, or for those who draw up a full Tree with all of the known ancestors on it. A picture can be worth a thousand words, and a word worth a thousand pictures.

In fact, if the research is your only talent, but you have family members with a particular skill.....well, it's their family too. A challenge, a reward, a twist of the arm, maybe a little begging, sighs of admiration at their skills...all worth a try.

Twist and Stretch.

That's not only what I'll need to do when I finish writing this, but it is also a further thought. If I might say to you what should a Tree for a butcher, baker, tinkerman or sailor look like, you'll probably envision cuts of meat and cleavers, bread and cakes, pots and pans, ships and seagulls....but now for the twist and stretch :

What might a Surrealist's Tree look like ? Would the boxes be melting ? How about a Heavy Metal or Jazz one ? A Cubist's one already sounds boxy, but a rebel's one ? A manic depressive's ? A Christian's ? An Architect's or a Doctor's or a Dutchman's or a Factory Worker's ? We really are all different though we may also have some common themes.

I hope that my books have at least cracked open a door enough for you to see what possibilities there are. Contact me if you need any suggestions. I'm just full of ideas, but I bet you folks will come up with some novel Trees too. Send me a photo.

Meanwhile....enjoy my feast, then treet yourself !

FAMILY PICNIC

© Tony Matthews 2000

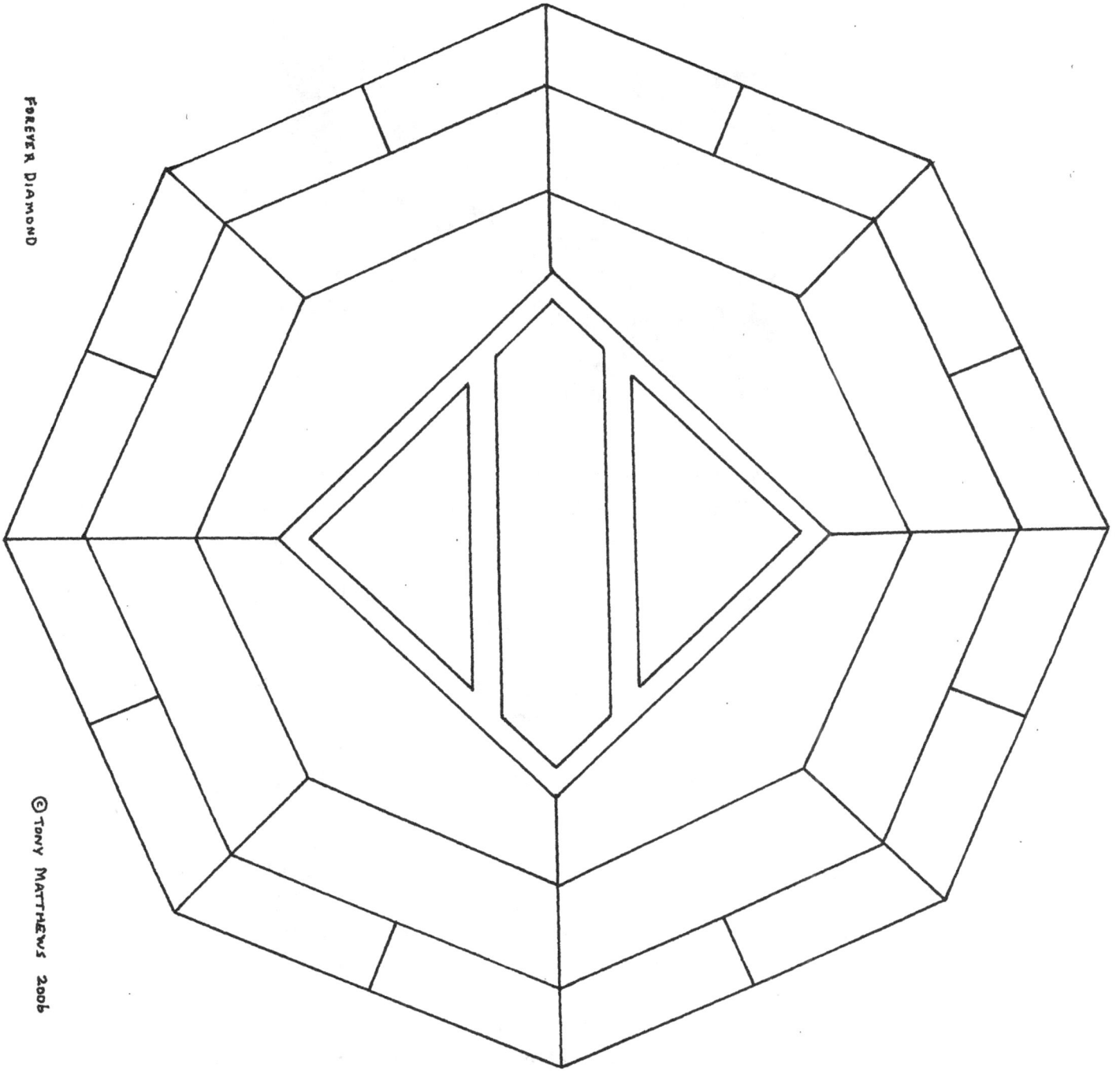

Tony Matthews was born on the 7th of May 1949, near
Bracknell in Berkshire, England. He is the second son of
George Matthews (the son of Edward Walter Matthews
and Louisa Matilda Lane) and Joyce Margery Cooke
(daughter of Ernest Cooke and Hilda Maud Lucas Keeble).
His roots are sunk in Bracknell, Chertsey in Surrey, London,
Ramsey in Essex, Stratford-Upon-Avon and Ireland. He's
had a very varied life (so far) with jobs that have included
research in Applied Entomology, factories, astrology,
gardening, house painting and decorating, door-door
selling.....all interspersed with roaming around Europe.
What else could he do then but become a Family Tree
Designer ? He says that it made sense at the time.
Homes have included Bracknell, London, Woodbridge
in Suffolk, and stays in Athens, and the Shetland Isles,
as well as San Antonio and Corpus Christi in Texas.
Currently he lives with his wife Linda Goetsch in
Gainesville, Texas, (after getting married at the Grand
Canyon), from where they run their Tree business as
Paper Tree, also using their website grillyourgranny.com
You are empowered to make copies of Tony's Trees for
your personal use, but not for profit or gain. For more
extensive uses, such as schools, please contact him.......
likewise if your creative juices run dry : you (or Tony)
have no idea what he will come up with next.